The Bahá'í Faith

A SHORT INTRODUCTION

OTHER BOOKS IN THIS SERIES

Buddhism: A Short History, Edward Conze, ISBN 1–85168–221–X
Buddhism: A Short Introduction, Klaus K. Klostermaier, ISBN 1–85168–186–8
The Buddha: A Short Biography, John S. Strong, ISBN 1–85168–256–2
Hinduism: A Short History, Klaus K. Klostermaier, ISBN 1–85168–213–9
Hindu Writings: A Short Introduction to the Major Sources, Klaus K. Klostermaier,
    ISBN 1–85168–230–9
Hinduism: A Short Introduction, Klaus K. Klostermaier, ISBN 1–85168–220–1
Islamic Philosophy, Theology and Mysticism: A Short Introduction, Majid Fakhry,
    ISBN 1–85168–252–X
Muhammad: A Short Biography, Martin Forward, ISBN 1–85168–131–0
Islam: A Short History, William Montgomery Watt, ISBN 1–85168–205–8
Islam: A Short Introduction, Abdulkader Tayob, ISBN 1–85168–192–2
The Qur'an: A Short Introduction, Farid Esack, ISBN 1–85168–231–7
Jesus: A Short Biography, Martin Forward, ISBN 1–85168–172–8
Christianity: A Short Introduction, Keith Ward, ISBN 1–85168–229–5
Christianity: A Short Global History, Frederick W. Norris, ISBN 1–85168–296–1
The New Testament: A Short Introduction, W.R. Telford, ISBN 1–85168–289–9
The Old Testament Prophets: A Short Introduction, E. W. Heaton,
    ISBN 1–85168–277–5
Judaism: A Short History, Lavinia and Dan Cohn-Sherbok, ISBN 1–85168–206–6
Judaism: A Short Introduction, Lavinia and Dan Cohn-Sherbok, ISBN 1–85168–207–4
Judaism: A Short Reader, Lavinia and Dan Cohn-Sherbok, ISBN 1–85168–278–3
Sufism: A Short Introduction, William C. Chittick, ISBN 1–85168–211–2
The Bahá'í Faith: A Short History, Peter Smith, ISBN 1–85168–208–2
Confucianism: A Short Introduction, John and Evelyn Berthrong, ISBN 1–85168–236–8
The Psychology of Religion: A Short Introduction, Kate M. Loewenthal,
    ISBN 1–85168–212–0
Pluralism in the World Religions: A Short Introduction, Harold Coward,
    ISBN 1–856168–243–0
Scripture in the World Religions: A Short Introduction, Harold Coward,
    ISBN 1–85168–244–9
Global Philosophy of Religion: A Short Introduction, Joseph Runzo,
    ISBN 1–85168–235–X
Inter-religious Dialogue: A Short Introduction, Martin Forward, ISBN 1–85168–275–9

The Bahá'í Faith

A SHORT INTRODUCTION

Moojan Momen

ONEWORLD
OXFORD

THE BAHÁ'Í FAITH: A SHORT INTRODUCTION

Oneworld Publications
(Sales and Editorial)
185 Banbury Road
Oxford OX2 7AR
England
www.oneworld-publications.com

ISBN 1–85168–209–0

Cover design by Design Deluxe, Bath
Printed and bound in England by Clays Ltd, St Ives plc

CONTENTS

INTRODUCTION   1

1 THE INDIVIDUAL   5

How can we be happy?   5
The spiritual quest   7
What are we and what is our purpose?   12
What we must become   13
Can we reach these goals?   20
The pursuit of freedom   21
Physical and spiritual health   23

2 THE FAMILY   25

Marriage   25
Children and family life   27
Education   29

3 SOCIETY   34

Freedom from prejudice   35
The advancement of women   37
Science, technology and the environment   40
Liberty and human rights   42
Agriculture   45
Teachings on government and social policy   45
Teachings on economics   48
General principles and other teachings   52

4 GLOBAL CONCERNS   54

The unity of humankind   54

World order   59
Social and economic development   63

5 THE BAHÁ'Í COMMUNITY   67

Structures   67
Principles of Bahá'í administration   75

6 BAHÁ'Í LAWS   83

Prayer, reading of scripture and meditation   84
Fasting   88
Marriage and divorce   88
Death and burial   89
Cruelty to animals   90
Abolitions and prohibitions   90

7 THEOLOGICAL TEACHINGS   91

The nature of the highest reality (God)   91
The divine educator, the Manifestation of God   95
True religion   97
The goal of human life (salvation)   103
The cause and purpose of suffering   108
Life after death   110

8 THE HISTORY OF THE BAHÁ'Í FAITH   115

The Báb   115
Bahá'u'lláh   119
'Abdu'l-Bahá   126
Shoghi Effendi   127
The Universal House of Justice   128

9 THE BAHÁ'Í WORLD TODAY   130

The expansion of the Bahá'í community   130
Co-operation with the United Nations and other
international agencies   134
Social and economic development projects   135
The Bahá'í community as a model   136

Notes   141
Bibliography   145
Further Reading   147
Further Information   149
Index   150

INTRODUCTION

In the brief course of its 150-year history, the Bahá'í Faith has transformed itself from a little-known Middle Eastern religious movement into a fast-growing global religion. Now established in every country of the world, it is rapidly emerging out of obscurity to take its place alongside older and more established world religions. In the course of its history, the religion has grown and developed greatly in terms of its numerical strength, geographical spread and community organization. The largest Bahá'í communities are now in South Asia, Africa, Latin America and (relative to the size of the population) in some of the islands of the Pacific. In these parts of the world, some villages and areas are more or less completely Bahá'í. Here the Bahá'ís have initiated educational, agricultural and community development projects. The latest available official Bahá'í statistics (1994) state that there are between five and six million Bahá'ís in the world; that Bahá'ís live in over 110,000 localities; that there are over 17,000 places where there are organized Bahá'í communities with elected local councils (Local Spiritual Assemblies); and 172 national elected bodies (National Spiritual Assemblies). This book is intended to be a short introduction to the history and teachings of the Bahá'í Faith for those who know very little about it.

Many people think of religion as an activity that is carried out in a church, a mosque, a synagogue or a temple. It comes into the way that we relate to other people and, of course, plays a prominent role at the important events in our lives: births, marriages and deaths. But for most people (even those who consider themselves religious) most of the time, religion has no impact on any other part of their lives or on the society in which they live. If you want to understand the Bahá'í Faith, however, you need to think differently about religion. The scope of the Bahá'í Faith is much wider than this. In the Bahá'í scriptures, as well as the theology and personal ethics that you would expect to find in a religious scripture, there are teachings on subjects such as social ethics, race issues, feminist issues, economics, global government and legal matters. Indeed it could be said that there are few areas of human life, at the individual, social or global levels, about which the Bahá'í Faith does not have something to say. It is not that there are specific policies and detailed regulations on these areas, but rather there are general principles upon which policies can be formulated in response to specific situations.

If we imagine our life as a room, then for most people, as they view the room of their life, there is one part of the room that is concerned with their family, a part of the room that is concerned with their friends and social acquaintances, a part that is concerned with their job and, if they are religious, a part that is concerned with religion. But the Bahá'í view of religion is not that it should be a separate compartment of our lives, but rather that it should affect every part of our lives. In our analogy, as we look at the room of our life, religion should be the glasses through which we look. It should affect everything we see.

Those who have studied the Bahá'í Faith have noted that its teachings are very much in tune with the concerns of the present day. Its social teachings include such principles as the equality of men and women and the need for world peace. In emphasizing its social teachings, however, there has been a tendency in writing about the Bahá'í Faith to reduce the significance of its spiritual and mystical aspects. And yet, however advanced the social teachings may have been when they were first given by the central figures of the Bahá'í Faith decades ago, the modern world has, to a large extent, caught up with them. It is the spiritual and mystical teachings that may now be the aspect of the Bahá'í Faith that is of most interest to those who come across it for the first time. It is for this reason that this book is presented in a way that is different from other introductory books on the Bahá'í Faith. The book opens with, and therefore emphasizes, the spiritual aspects of Bahá'í teaching.

Partly because of its belief in the fundamental oneness of religion, some have called the Bahá'í Faith an eclectic or syncretic religion, one that gathers together the best aspects of the other religions. Since Bahá'ís believe that all religion emanates from the same spiritual source, they also consider it inevitable that all religions, including the Bahá'í Faith, will, to some extent, contain echoes of each other. In this book, however, I hope to show that the Bahá'í Faith also has its own teachings that are in many respects new and innovative.

Since the names of the central figures of the Bahá'í Faith will crop up frequently in the following pages, I will introduce them briefly here (more historical details can be found in chapter 8). The Bahá'í Faith began 150 years ago in Iran (Persia). It had its origins in the religious teachings of a young Iranian merchant named the Báb. His movement threw Iran into turmoil between 1844 and 1853. Out of this turmoil emerged the Bahá'í Faith, which was founded by Bahá'u'lláh, an Iranian nobleman who was at first imprisoned for his support for the Báb. He then went, in 1853, into the first of a series of exiles that culminated in his arrival in 1868 in Akka, which was then a prison-city in the Ottoman Turkish Empire. Bahá'u'lláh remained in Akka and its vicinity, elaborating the teachings of his religion, until his death in 1892.

Bahá'u'lláh appointed his son 'Abdu'l-Bahá as the leader of the Bahá'í community and the authorized interpreter of his teachings. After he was freed in 1909 from the restrictions imposed upon him by his imprisonment and exile, 'Abdu'l-Bahá travelled to Egypt, Europe and North America, helping to make a firm foundation for the Bahá'í Faith in those regions.

When 'Abdu'l-Bahá died in 1921, he appointed his grandson, Shoghi Effendi, as the next leader of the Bahá'í Faith and the authorized interpreter of the Bahá'í teachings. Shoghi Effendi is often referred to by his title, the Guardian of the Bahá'í Faith. He died in 1957. In 1963, the first international election was held for the Universal House of Justice, which is now the international governing body of the Bahá'í Faith. It operates from the world centre of the Bahá'í Faith in the Haifa–Akka area, now in the state of Israel.

The teachings and institutional foundations of the Bahá'í Faith are derived from the writings of Bahá'u'lláh, 'Abdu'l-Bahá, and Shoghi Effendi. The Universal House of Justice is empowered to legislate on any areas that are not expressly covered in these texts.

During the 150 years of its history, the Bahá'í Faith has spread to all parts of the world. There are now Bahá'í communities in every country and Bahá'í literature has been published in all major languages. One of the fascinating features of the Bahá'í Faith is the way in which it has been successful in attracting large numbers of people from every conceivable background. In its country of origin, it attracted many thousands of Iranians from a Muslim background in both rural and urban areas; from there it spread to North America where large numbers of urban Christians became Bahá'ís; in South America, hundreds of thousands of Amerindian peasants from a Roman Catholic background have been converted; in India, over two million Hindu villagers have become Bahá'ís; in South-East Asia, large numbers of Buddhists have become Bahá'ís. In all, the Bahá'í Faith is now regarded by authoritative independent sources as the second most widespread religion after Christianity – only the Roman Catholic Church is more widespread. Some of the reasons for the fact that the Bahá'í Faith has proved so attractive to such a wide array of humanity will, I hope, emerge from a reading of this book.

I have not attempted to provide a historical analysis of the way in which the Bahá'í Faith, and in particular its administrative structure, has evolved historically. One of the main features of the Bahá'í Faith is the rapid evolution that it has undergone. This has occurred within the framework laid down by its founder and his successors and in response to changes in its situation and in world conditions. In the limited space available in this book, all that I can do is to present a snapshot of the point to which the religion has evolved at the present time.

In some instances, the quotations in this book have been laid out differently from the original text in order to improve clarity.

Moojan Momen

1 THE INDIVIDUAL

Many people spend a great deal of time wondering about the meaning of their lives. Is there any purpose to my life? If there is a purpose, how can I discover it and how can I fulfil that purpose? How can I achieve a lasting happiness and contentment?

HOW CAN WE BE HAPPY?

At present, we are inundated with claims about what will make us happy and contented human beings. How often do we read in the newspapers that someone who claims to be an authority has asserted that if only we would do such-and-such a thing, we would be happy? How often do we see on the television an advertisement that claims that if only we would buy some product, we would be content? Examples of business executives, film stars, sports personalities and pop stars are paraded in front of us as people who have 'made it', are successful, have everything that our society can offer, and are therefore presumably happy and content. Yet we know, from those same newspapers, magazines and television programmes that, so often, the pictures presented to us of successful people hide loneliness, despair and frustration. Power and wealth are presented to us as worthwhile goals, as a measure of a person's success and value to society. And yet at the same time, we know that those who attain these goals are often people who may have difficulty relating to others, who may be emotionally and spiritually impoverished, and are therefore unable to enjoy what they have achieved.

Bahá'u'lláh's writings indicate that, if we want happiness and contentment, we must do precisely the opposite to what we are constantly being urged to do by many of those around us. He advises us: 'Dissipate not the wealth of your precious lives in the pursuit of evil and corrupt affection, nor let your endeavours be spent in promoting your personal interest.'[1] Referring to the illusion that wealth is of itself of any value to human happiness and development, Bahá'u'lláh says: 'Thou dost wish for gold and I desire thy freedom from it. Thou thinkest thyself rich in its possession, and I recognize thy wealth in thy sanctity therefrom. By My life! This is My knowledge, and that is thy fancy; how can My way accord with thine?'[2]

◆

THE FUTILITY OF OUR QUEST FOR WEALTH

'Abdu'l-Bahá cites the animals as an example of the futility of our quest for wealth and power:

A bird, on the summit of a mountain, on the high, waving branches, has built for itself a nest more beautiful than the palaces of the kings! The air is in the utmost purity, the water cool and clear as crystal, the panorama charming and enchanting. In such glorious surroundings, he expends his numbered days. All the harvests of the plain are his possessions, having earned all this wealth without the least labour. Hence, no matter how much man may advance in this world, he shall not attain to the station of this bird!

Thus it becomes evident that in the matters of this world, however much man may strive and work to the point of death, he will be unable to earn the abundance, the freedom and the independent life of a small bird. This proves and establishes the fact that man is not created for the life of this ephemeral world: – nay, rather, is he created for the acquirement of infinite perfections, for the attainment to the sublimity of the world of humanity, to be drawn nigh unto the divine threshold, and to sit on the throne of everlasting sovereignty!

Tablets of the Divine Plan, pp. 42–3

◆

Our belief that we can gain happiness by accumulating wealth and power or by indulging our sensual or material passions is due to the fact that we have been deluded by the physical world that surrounds us. It seems so immediate and 'real' that we think that it is the most important thing. The pressing immediacy and vividness of this world are, however, veils hiding its emptiness. According to Bahá'u'lláh:

The world is but a show, vain and empty, a mere nothing, bearing the semblance of reality. Set not your affections upon it . . . Verily I say, the world is like the vapour in a desert, which the thirsty dreameth to be water and striveth after it with all his might, until when he cometh unto it, he findeth it to be mere illusion.[3]

Elsewhere in the Bahá'í scriptures our life in this world is compared to a passing wave on the surface of the ocean or a fleeting shadow.[4] This world and all that it promises are with us for only a short time. We should not therefore grow attached to what will eventually fade and wither away:

These few brief days shall pass away, this present life shall vanish from our sight; the roses of this world shall be fresh and fair no more, the garden of this earth's triumphs and delights shall droop and fade. The spring season of life shall turn into the autumn of death, the bright joy of palace halls give way to moonless dark within the tomb. And therefore is none of this worth loving at all, and to this the wise will not anchor his heart. ('Abdu'l-Bahá)[5]

It is the nature of this physical world to be full of pain and suffering:

Such is this mortal abode: a storehouse of afflictions and suffering. It is ignorance that binds man to it, for no comfort can be secured by any soul in this world, from monarch down to the most humble commoner. If once this life should offer a man a sweet cup, a hundred bitter ones will follow; such is the condition of this world. ('Abdu'l-Bahá)[6]

We should try to change ourselves before the short time that we have on this earth comes to an end.[7] Bahá'u'lláh urges us to cut ourselves free from the attractions of this world and the pursuit of selfish aims: 'O My Servant! Free thyself from the fetters of this world, and loose thy soul from the prison of self. Seize thy chance, for it will come to thee no more.'[8]

THE SPIRITUAL QUEST

If we are to find and understand the knowledge that leads to lasting happiness and contentment, we must search for it. Our search, however, must not be among the things of this world, which only lead to sadness and suffering; rather, we must make our search a spiritual quest. Bahá'u'lláh has likened the search to a spiritual journey and he has described the standard that must be achieved if the journey is to be successful.

The first condition for success in the search is patience and perseverance: 'Without patience the wayfarer on this journey will reach

---◆---

THE TRUE SEEKER AND THE SEARCH

But, O my brother, when a true seeker determineth to take the step of search in the path leading to the knowledge of the Ancient of Days, he must, before all else, cleanse and purify his heart . . . from the obscuring dust of all acquired knowledge, and the allusions of the embodiments of satanic fancy. He must purge his breast . . . of every defilement, and sanctify his soul from all that pertaineth to water and clay, from all shadowy and ephemeral attachments. He must so cleanse his heart that no remnant of either love or hate may linger therein, lest that love blindly incline him to error, or that hate repel him away from the truth . . . That seeker must at all times put his trust in God, must renounce the peoples of the earth, detach himself from the world of dust, and cleave unto Him Who is the Lord of Lords. He must never seek to exalt himself above any one, must wash away from the tablet of his heart every trace of pride and vainglory, must cling unto patience and resignation, observe silence, and refrain from idle talk . . .

That seeker should also regard backbiting as grievous error, and keep himself aloof from its dominion, inasmuch as backbiting quencheth the light of the heart, and extinguisheth the life of the soul. He should be content with little, and be freed from all inordinate desire. He should treasure the companionship of those that have renounced the world, and regard avoidance of boastful and worldly people a precious benefit. At the dawn of every day he should commune with God, and with all his soul persevere in the quest of his Beloved. He should consume every wayward thought with the flame of His loving mention, and, with the swiftness of lightning, pass by all else save Him. He should succour the dispossessed, and never withhold his favour from the destitute. He should show kindness to animals, how much more unto his fellow-man, to him who is endowed with the power of utterance. He should not hesitate to offer up his life for his Beloved, nor allow the censure of the people to turn him away from the Truth. He should not wish for others that which he doth not wish for himself, nor promise that which he doth not fulfill. With all his heart should the seeker avoid fellowship with evil doers, and pray for the remission of their sins. He should forgive the sinful, and never despise his low estate, for none knoweth what his own end shall be . . .

Only when the lamp of search, of earnest striving, of longing desire, of passionate devotion, of fervid love, of rapture, and ecstasy, is kindled within the seeker's heart, and the breeze of His loving-kindness is wafted upon his soul, will the darkness of error be dispelled, the mists of doubts and misgivings be dissipated, and the lights of knowledge and certitude envelop his being. At that hour will the mystic Herald, bearing the joyful tidings of the Spirit, shine forth from the City of God resplendent as the morn, and, through the trumpet blast of knowledge, will awaken the heart, the soul, and the spirit from the slumber of negligence. Then will the manifold favours and outpouring grace of the holy and everlasting Spirit confer such new life upon the seeker that he will find himself endowed with a new eye, a new ear, a new heart, and a new mind. He will contemplate the manifest signs of the universe, and will penetrate the hidden mysteries of the soul. Gazing with the eye of God, he will perceive within every atom a door that leadeth him to the stations of absolute certitude. He will discover in all things the mysteries of divine Revelation and the evidences of an everlasting manifestation.

I swear by God! Were he that treadeth the path of guidance and seeketh to scale the heights of righteousness to attain unto this glorious and supreme station, he would inhale at a distance of a thousand leagues the fragrance of God, and would perceive the resplendent morn of a divine Guidance rising above the dayspring of all things. Each and every thing, however small, would be to him a revelation, leading him to his Beloved, the Object of his quest. So great shall be the discernment of this seeker that he will discriminate between truth and falsehood even as he doth distinguish the sun from shadow... He will likewise clearly distinguish all the signs of God – His wondrous utterances, His great works, and mighty deeds – from the doings, words and ways of men, even as the jeweller who knoweth the gem from the stone, or the man who distinguisheth the spring from autumn and heat from cold. When the channel of the human soul is cleansed of all worldly and impeding attachments, it will unfailingly perceive the breath of the Beloved across immeasurable distances, and will, led by its perfume, attain and enter the City of Certitude. Therein he will discern the wonders of His ancient wisdom, and will perceive all the hidden teachings from the rustling leaves of the Tree – which flourisheth in that City.

Bahá'u'lláh, *Kitáb-i-Íqán*, pp. 192–8

◆

nowhere and attain no goal. Nor should he ever be downhearted; if he strive for a hundred thousand years and yet fail to behold the beauty of the Friend, he should not falter.'[9]

The second condition for success is to search with an open mind. We must be ready to set aside our fondest ideas and our preconceived notions:

It is incumbent on these servants that they cleanse the heart – which is the wellspring of divine treasures – from every marking, and that they turn away from imitation, which is following the traces of their forefathers and sires . . . Nor shall the seeker reach his goal unless he sacrifice all things. That is, whatever he hath seen, and heard, and understood, all must he set at naught, that he may enter the realm of the spirit, which is the City of God.[10]

The third condition is an intense desire for the goal of the quest, an

THE VALLEY OF KNOWLEDGE

There was once a lover who had sighed for long years in separation from his beloved, and wasted in the fire of remoteness. From the rule of love, his heart was empty of patience, and his body weary of his spirit; he reckoned life without her as a mockery, and time consumed him away. How many a day he found no rest in longing for her; how many a night the pain of her kept him from sleep; his body was worn to a sigh, his heart's wound had turned him to a cry of sorrow. He had given a thousand lives for one taste of the cup of her presence, but it availed him not. The doctors knew no cure for him, and companions avoided his company; yea, physicians have no medicine for one sick of love, unless the favour of the beloved one deliver him.

At last, the tree of his longing yielded the fruit of despair, and the fire of his hope fell to ashes. Then one night he could live no more, and he went out of his house and made for the marketplace. On a sudden, a watchman followed after him. He broke into a run, with the watchman following; then other watchmen came together, and barred every passage to the weary one. And the wretched one cried from his heart, and ran here and there, and moaned to himself: 'Surely this watchman is Izra'il, my angel of death, following so fast upon me; or he is a tyrant of men, seeking to harm me.' His feet carried him on, the one bleeding with the arrow of love, and his heart lamented. Then he came to a garden wall, and with untold pain he scaled it, for it proved very high; and forgetting his life, he threw himself down to the garden.

And there he beheld his beloved with a lamp in her hand, searching for a ring she had lost. When the heart-surrendered lover looked on his ravishing love, he drew a great breath and raised up his hands in prayer, crying: 'O God! Give Thou glory to the watchman, and riches and long life. For the watchman was Gabriel, guiding this poor one; or he was Israfil, bringing life to this wretched one!'

Indeed, his words were true, for he had found many a secret justice in this seeming tyranny of the watchman, and seen how many a mercy lay hid behind the veil. Out of wrath, the guard had led him who was athirst in love's desert to the sea of his loved one, and lit up the dark night of absence with the light of reunion. He had driven one who was afar, into the garden of nearness, had guided an ailing soul to the heart's physician.

Now if the lover could have looked ahead, he would have blessed the watchman at the start, and prayed on his behalf, and he would have seen that tyranny as justice; but since the end was veiled to him, he moaned and made his plaint in the beginning. Yet those who journey in the garden land of knowledge, because they see the end in the beginning, see peace in war and friendliness in anger.

Bahá'u'lláh, *Seven Valleys*, pp. 13–15

ardour or burning passion to achieve the objective. For the journey may be long and hard and there will be the many distractions of our daily lives to tempt us away:

> The true seeker hunteth naught but the object of his quest, and the lover hath no desire save union with his beloved . . . Labour is needed, if we are to seek Him; ardour is needed, if we are to drink of the honey of reunion with Him; and if we taste of this cup, we shall cast away the world.
>
> On this journey the traveller abideth in every land and dwelleth in every region. In every face, he seeketh the beauty of the Friend; in every country he looketh for the Beloved. He joineth every company, and seeketh fellowship with every soul, that haply in some mind he may uncover the secret of the Friend, or in some face he may behold the beauty of the Loved One.[11]

Our first step on the path is to detach ourselves from the attractions of this physical world. It is our clinging to these things of the physical world that blinds us to spiritual reality and holds back our spiritual progress. We must try to free ourselves from this: 'Disencumber yourselves of all attachment to this world and the vanities thereof. Beware that ye approach them not, inasmuch as they prompt you to walk after your own lusts and covetous desires, and hinder you from entering the straight and glorious Path' (Bahá'u'lláh).[12] All of these possessions on which we pride ourselves are transient.[13] Bahá'u'lláh advises us: 'Abandon not the everlasting beauty for a beauty that must die, and set not your affections on this mortal world of dust.'[14]

It is not only the physical things of this world to which we cling. Bahá'u'lláh also calls upon people to shatter 'the idols of their vain imaginings'.[15]

> Even as the swiftness of lightning ye have passed by the Beloved One, and have set your hearts on satanic fancies. Ye bow the knee before your vain imagining, and call it truth. Ye turn your eyes towards the thorn, and name it a flower. Not a pure breath have ye breathed, nor hath the breeze of detachment been wafted from the meadows of your hearts. Ye have cast to the winds the loving counsels of the Beloved and have effaced them utterly from the tablet of your hearts, and even as the beasts of the field, ye move and have your being within the pastures of desire and passion.[16]

The process of detaching ourselves from our love for the attractions of this world is, however, a painful one. It is for this reason that

Bahá'u'lláh says that if our hearts are attracted by love for the spiritual world then our companion in the course of our spiritual journey is pain. And yet this pain, because its result is joy and contentment, should be welcomed:

> Love setteth a world aflame at every turn, and he wasteth every land where he carrieth his banner . . . He hath bound a myriad victims in his fetters, wounded a myriad wise men with his arrow. Know that every redness in the world is from his anger, and every paleness in men's cheeks is from his poison. He yieldeth no remedy but death, he walketh not save in the valley of the shadow; yet sweeter than honey is his venom on the lover's lips, and fairer his destruction in the seeker's eyes than a hundred thousand lives.[17]

This pain, Bahá'u'lláh says, is caused by the burning away of the veils of illusion that have kept us bound to this world and away from the spiritual world. It is through this burning that the spirit is purified and a love arises for the spiritual world.[18] Once these veils have been removed, then we see the world with different eyes; we discern a new meaning in the events of our lives and in everything around us:

> His inner eyes will open and he will privily converse with his Beloved; he will set ajar the gate of truth and piety, and shut the doors of vain imaginings. He . . . seeth war as peace, and findeth in death the secrets of everlasting life . . . He beholdeth justice in injustice, and in justice, grace. In ignorance he findeth many a knowledge hidden, and in knowledge a myriad wisdoms manifest. He breaketh the cage of the body and the passions, and consorteth with the people of the immortal realm . . . And if he meeteth with injustice he shall have patience, and if he cometh upon wrath he shall manifest love.[19]

WHAT ARE WE AND WHAT IS OUR PURPOSE?

What is the reason that we are upon the earth? What is the purpose of our lives here? Such questions have been the theme of the meditations and speculations of many philosophers and religious leaders down the ages. To understand the Bahá'í view on such questions, however, it is necessary to examine first the Bahá'í teachings on the true nature of a human being.

It has become fashionable for scientists and philosophers to emphasize how close we, as human beings, are to the animal world. So many of our human characteristics can also be found among the animals, and in particular among the monkeys and apes. The Bahá'í scriptures assert, however, that the human being is spiritually a different order of being from the animal. Bahá'u'lláh says that, whereas everything in creation is capable of reflecting some of the divine attributes, human beings alone have the capacity to reflect them all:

> Upon the inmost reality of each and every created thing He hath shed the light of one of His names, and made it a recipient of the glory of one of His attributes. Upon the reality of man, however, He hath focused the radiance of all of His names and attributes, and made it a mirror of His own Self. Alone of all created things man hath been singled out for so great a favour, so enduring a bounty.[20]

Our purpose in life, therefore, is to develop this potential and show these divine attributes in our actions; our purpose is 'the attainment of the supreme virtues of humanity through descent of the heavenly bestowals' ('Abdu'l-Bahá).[21]

During our lives here on earth, then, we must try to acquire as many of these divine attributes as possible and to perfect them. Human beings have two sides to their nature, a lower aspect which is concerned with the material or animal side of our life, and a higher aspect which is the spiritual side. It is this second higher aspect that makes us truly human. 'Abdu'l-Bahá says that we must constantly struggle to ensure that our higher side overcomes our animal side: 'Then if the divine power in man, which is his essential perfection, overcomes the satanic power, which is absolute imperfection, he becomes the most excellent among the creatures; but if the satanic power overcomes the divine power, he becomes the lowest of the creatures.'[22]

WHAT WE MUST BECOME

What are these virtues that we must acquire to become truly human, to achieve lasting contentment and happiness? They are numerous and, as they cannot all be considered here, we will briefly review a few of the most important.

Justice

Bahá'u'lláh places great importance on our developing justice as a personal quality. The ability to be just and equitable in our assessment of situations and in our dealings with others is reckoned by Bahá'u'lláh as the 'most fundamental among human virtues'. This is because 'the evaluation of all things must needs depend upon it'.[23] Therefore, 'the essence of all that We have revealed for thee is Justice, is for man to free himself from idle fancy and imitation, discern with the eye of oneness His glorious handiwork, and look into all things with a searching eye.'[24]

Bahá'u'lláh states that 'the best beloved of all things in My sight is Justice'. For:

> By its aid thou shalt see with thine own eyes and not through the eyes of others, and shalt know of thine own knowledge and not through the knowledge of thy neighbour. Ponder this in thy heart; how it behooveth thee to be. Verily justice is My gift to thee and the sign of My loving-kindness. Set it then before thine eyes.[25]

Part of justice is being fair in the way that one treats others: to choose 'for thy neighbour that which thou choosest for thyself' (Bahá'u'lláh);[26] not 'to deny any soul the reward due to him' (Bahá'u'lláh);[27] and 'to respect the rights of all men' ('Abdu'l-Bahá).[28]

Love

Human beings have a great capacity for love. 'Abdu'l-Bahá says that 'there are many ways of expressing the love principle; there is love for the family, for the country, for the race, there is political enthusiasm . . . These are all ways and means of showing the power of love.' He warns, however, that these expressions of love are of a limited nature and may in fact also arouse hate:

> The love of family is limited . . . Frequently members of the same family disagree, and even hate each other. Patriotic love is finite; the love of one's country causing hatred of all others, is not perfect love! . . . The love of race is limited . . . To love our own race may mean hatred of all others, and even people of the same race often dislike each other . . . Political love also is much bound up with hatred of one party for another . . . All these ties of love are imperfect. It is clear that limited material ties are insufficient to adequately express the universal love.[29]

Real love, the spiritual love to which human beings should aspire, should be unlimited and universal:

> Love is unlimited, boundless, infinite! Material things are limited, circumscribed, finite. You cannot adequately express infinite love by limited means. The perfect love needs an unselfish instrument, absolutely freed from fetters of every kind . . . The great unselfish love for humanity is bounded by none of these imperfect, semi-selfish bonds; this is the one perfect love, possible to all mankind, and can only be achieved by the power of the Divine Spirit. No worldly power can accomplish the universal love.[30]

Associated with love are several other qualities that Bahá'u'lláh praises and that should govern our relations with others. Among these are kindliness, friendliness, compassion, charity, forbearence and generosity. There are many statements from Bahá'u'lláh and 'Abdu'l-Bahá about these qualities. The following are a few examples:

> Consort with all men, O people of Bahá, in a spirit of friendliness and fellowship. (Bahá'u'lláh)[31]

> Let them at all times concern themselves with doing a kindly thing for one of their fellows, offering to someone love, consideration, thoughtful help. Let them see no one as their enemy, or as wishing them ill, but think of all humankind as their friends; regarding the alien as an intimate, the stranger as a companion, staying free of prejudice, drawing no lines. ('Abdu'l-Bahá)[32]

> It is incumbent upon the loved ones of God to exercise the greatest care and prudence in all things . . . They must endeavour to consort in a friendly spirit with everyone, must follow moderation in their conduct, must have respect and consideration one for another and show loving-kindness and tender regard to all the peoples of the world. They must be patient and long-suffering. ('Abdu'l-Bahá)[33]

Trustworthiness and truthfulness

Trustworthiness is the basis for all of human social life. In the writings of Bahá'u'lláh, it is accorded great importance since 'the stability of every affair hath depended and doth depend upon it'.[34] It is described as 'the door of security for all that dwell on earth', 'the greatest portal leading unto the tranquillity and security of the people'[35] and the 'supreme instrument for the prosperity of the world'.[36]

Truthfulness is the 'foundation of all human virtues' (Bahá'u'lláh).[37] This is because, together with justice, it protects us from self-deception and enables us to measure our spiritual progress. It forestalls hypocrisy and insincerity: 'Beautify your tongues, O people, with truthfulness, and adorn your souls with the ornament of honesty. Beware, O people, that ye deal not treacherously with any one' (Bahá'u'lláh).[38] Part of the truthfulness and sincerity that Bahá'u'lláh advocates is for his followers to act in accordance with the high ideals that they profess (see pp. 18–19 below).

Purity and chastity

The pursuit of a self-centred and self-indulgent lifestyle is condemned by Bahá'u'lláh because it does not lead to human happiness.

> Like the bats of darkness, they lift not their heads from their couch except to pursue the transient things of the world, and find no rest by night except as they labour to advance the aims of their sordid life . . . In the day-time they strive with all their soul after worldly benefits, and in the night-season their sole occupation is to gratify their carnal desires.[39]

Purity is not a word that is fashionable in the world today. To a person who is struggling to develop spiritually, it signifies the attempt to free oneself from self-interest, from the corruption and degeneracy of the modern world, and from such base instincts as envy, malice, pride, lust, hypocrisy and hatred. The aim, however, is not to achieve a haughty puritanism or to become priggish; nor is a severe asceticism considered desirable:

> It must be remembered, however, that the maintenance of such a high standard of moral conduct is not to be associated or confused with any form of asceticism, or of excessive and bigoted puritanism. The standard inculcated by Bahá'u'lláh, seeks, under no circumstances, to deny anyone the legitimate right and privilege to derive the fullest advantage and benefit from the manifold joys, beauties, and pleasures with which the world has been so plentifully enriched by an All-Loving Creator. (Shoghi Effendi)[40]

To advance along the road of purity frees us from the insistent demands of our lower nature. Since these demands can never be satisfied, advancing along this path in fact leads to freedom and contentment:

Live then the days of thy life, that are less than a fleeting moment, with thy mind stainless, thy heart unsullied, thy thoughts pure, and thy nature sanctified, so that, free and content, thou mayest put away this mortal frame, and repair unto the mystic paradise and abide in the eternal kingdom for evermore. (Bahá'u'lláh)[41]

◆

PURITY AND CHASTITY

Such a chaste and holy life, with its implications of modesty, purity, temperance, decency, and clean-mindedness, involves no less than the exercise of moderation in all that pertains to dress, language, amusements, and all artistic and literary avocations. It demands daily vigilance in the control of one's carnal desires and corrupt inclinations. It calls for the abandonment of a frivolous conduct, with its excessive attachment to trivial and often misdirected pleasures . . . It can tolerate no compromise with the theories, the standards, the habits, and the excesses of a decadent age. Nay rather it seeks to demonstrate, through the dynamic force of its example, the pernicious character of such theories, the falsity of such standards, the hollowness of such claims, the perversity of such habits, and the sacrilegious character of such excesses.

Shoghi Effendi, *Advent of Divine Justice*, p. 30

◆

Chastity is the sexual aspect of purity. Again it should not be mistaken for prudery or the suppression of sexuality. It is rather the acknowledgement that the sexual instinct is strong and requires some degree of conscious control:

The Bahá'í Faith recognizes the value of the sex impulse, but condemns its illegitimate and improper expressions such as free love, companionate marriage and others, all of which it considers positively harmful to man and to the society in which he lives. The proper use of the sex instinct is the natural right of every individual, and it is precisely for this purpose that the institution of marriage has been established. The Bahá'ís do not believe in the suppression of the sex impulse but in its regulation and control. (Shoghi Effendi)[42]

This control should ideally extend not just to actions but even to one's thoughts: 'And if he met the fairest and most comely of women, he would not feel his heart seduced by the least shadow of desire for her beauty. Such an one, indeed, is the creation of spotless chastity' (Bahá'u'lláh).[43]

Actions not words

The Bahá'í writings emphasize that the result of our efforts on the spiritual path must be seen in our character and our actions. Bahá'u'lláh calls upon his followers to match their actions to their words: 'Let deeds,

◆

A SUMMARY OF VIRTUE

Be generous in prosperity, and thankful in adversity.
Be worthy of the trust of thy neighbour, and look upon him with a bright and friendly face.
Be a treasure to the poor,
    an admonisher to the rich,
    an answerer of the cry of the needy,
    a preserver of the sanctity of thy pledge.
Be fair in thy judgment, and guarded in thy speech.
Be unjust to no man, and show all meekness to all men.
Be as a lamp unto them that walk in darkness,
    a joy to the sorrowful,
    a sea for the thirsty,
    a haven for the distressed,
    an upholder and defender of the victim of oppression.
Let integrity and uprightness distinguish all thine acts.
Be a home for the stranger,
    a balm to the suffering,
    a tower of strength for the fugitive.
Be eyes to the blind, and a guiding light unto the feet of the erring.
Be an ornament to the countenance of truth,
    a crown to the brow of fidelity,
    a pillar of the temple of righteousness,
    a breath of life to the body of mankind,
    an ensign of the hosts of justice,
    a luminary above the horizon of virtue,
    a dew to the soil of the human heart,
    an ark on the ocean of knowledge,
    a sun in the heaven of bounty,
    a gem on the diadem of wisdom,
    a shining light in the firmament of thy generation,
    a fruit upon the tree of humility.

Bahá'u'lláh, *Gleanings*, no. 130, p. 285

◆

not words, be your adorning.'[44] It is easy for anyone to speak pious words and to utter sanctimonious platitudes. But Bahá'u'lláh says that 'the essence of faith is fewness of words and abundance of deeds'.[45] What distinguishes the person who is truly advancing on the spiritual path is their character and their actions:

> Guidance hath ever been given by words, and now it is given by deeds. Every one must show forth deeds that are pure and holy, for words are the property of all alike, whereas such deeds as these belong only to Our loved ones. Strive then with heart and soul to distinguish yourselves by your deeds.[46]

As has already been said, these Bahá'í teachings should not be regarded as advocating asceticism or a rigid puritanism. Both Bahá'u'lláh and 'Abdu'l-Bahá are recorded as having enjoyed laughter and joking. Bahá'u'lláh has even said that we can enjoy the things of this world as long as we do not allow them to come between us and our quest for the spiritual and the divine:

> Should a man wish to adorn himself with the ornaments of the earth, to wear its apparels, or partake of the benefits it can bestow, no harm can befall him, if he alloweth nothing whatever to intervene between him and God, for God hath ordained every good thing, whether created in the heavens or in the earth, for such of His servants as truly believe in Him. Eat ye, O people, of the good things which God hath allowed you, and deprive not yourselves from His wondrous bounties.[47]

Service

One important attribute, one characteristic that distinguishes those who are truly developing their human and spiritual characteristics, is their willingness and ability to serve others. It is, as Bahá'u'lláh has said, the characteristic of being truly human: 'That one indeed is a man who, today, dedicateth himself to the service of the entire human race. The Great Being saith: Blessed and happy is he that ariseth to promote the best interests of the peoples and kindreds of the earth.'[48]

Part of our service is the work that we do to earn our living. Bahá'u'lláh makes it a duty for all his followers to engage in some useful occupation and raises the status of such work to the level of worship:

It is enjoined upon each one of you to engage in some occupation, such as a craft, a trade or the like. We have exalted your engagement in such work to the rank of worship . . . Waste not your hours in idleness and sloth, but occupy yourselves with what will profit you and others.[49]

◆

SERVICE TO OTHERS

The following is a story about Lua Getsinger, an American Bahá'í who visited 'Abdu'l-Bahá in Akka.

She was with him one day when he said to her that he was too busy that day to call upon a friend of his who was very ill and poor. He wished her to go in his place. Take him food and care for him as I have been doing, he concluded. He told her where this man was to be found and she went gladly, proud that 'Abdu'l-Bahá should entrust her with this mission.

She returned quickly. 'Master,' she exclaimed, 'surely you cannot realize to what a terrible place you sent me. I almost fainted from the awful stench, the filthy rooms, the degrading condition of that man and his house. I fled lest I contract some terrible disease.'

Sadly and sternly 'Abdu'l-Bahá regarded her. 'Dost thou desire to serve God,' he said, 'serve thy fellow man for in him dost thou see the image and likeness of God.' He told her to go back to this man's house. If it is filthy, she should clean it; if this brother of yours is dirty, bathe him; if he is hungry, feed him. Do not return until this is done. Many times had he done this for him and cannot she serve him once?

Adapted from Ives, *Portals to Freedom*, p. 85

◆

CAN WE REACH THESE GOALS?

Some may question whether these goals that Bahá'u'lláh has set are too high and whether Bahá'ís are being too idealistic in trying to pursue them. Others may assert that the path that Bahá'u'lláh describes is too austere and sombre a way of life for most people.

There can be no intellectual answer to such objections. It is only by the experience of trying to live according to these teachings that one can see whether these objections have any basis or not. In writing of the need to plunge oneself into the experience to know what it is like rather than to stand on the edge observing, Bahá'u'lláh relates:

The story is told of a mystic knower, who went on a journey with a learned grammarian as his companion. They came to the shore of the Sea of Grandeur. The knower straightway flung himself into the waves, but the grammarian stood lost in his reasonings, which were as words that are written on water. The knower called out to him, 'Why dost thou not follow?' The grammarian answered, 'O Brother, I dare not advance. I must needs go back again.' Then the knower cried, 'Forget what thou didst read in . . . books . . . and cross the water.'[50]

Bahá'u'lláh does not expect human beings to be perfect from the outset, only that we take the first step and advance little by little. The path is long, hard and narrow, and Bahá'u'lláh has said that patience and perseverance are needed and that some degree of pain is inevitable (see pp. 7, 12). Bahá'u'lláh has, however, promised guidance and support from the spiritual world for those who seek to follow it. Part of this guidance and support comes from such spiritual exercises as prayer and meditation (see pp. 84–7). If we live with our thoughts concentrated upon the spiritual world, then the misfortunes and difficulties that we experience do not affect us, for there is an underlying contentment and joy:

> The trials which beset our every step, all our sorrow, pain, shame and grief, are born in the world of matter; whereas the spiritual Kingdom never causes sadness. A man living with his thoughts in this Kingdom knows perpetual joy. The ills all flesh is heir to do not pass him by, but they only touch the surface of his life, the depths are calm and serene. ('Abdu'l-Bahá)[51]

THE PURSUIT OF FREEDOM

The desire of individuals to be free to express and develop themselves has been one of the most persistent themes of this century. To a certain extent, it has been a natural reaction to the political, social and intellectual tyranny and oppression that much of humanity has suffered in the past (and in many parts of the world continues to suffer) at the hands of a small elite.

Bahá'u'lláh teaches that, for human beings, true freedom of the spirit arises from being free from captivity to our own animal nature. Of course, we cannot completely ignore the needs of the animal side of our nature, such needs as food, warmth, shelter, etc. If, however, we are constantly striving to satisfy these needs, if we allow that side of our being to dictate our actions, then we are nothing more than animals;

n some respects we are less, because unlike animals human
n choose to make more of their lives. And yet we find around us
people who do nothing more than spend their time in activities
designed in one way or another to satisfy their animal needs. It may seem
to them that they will achieve happiness in this way. In reality, however,
they are only feeding and cultivating the side of them that leads to pride,
arrogance, ambition, greed and sensual passions. This animal side can
never be satiated. However much an individual has of the things of this
world, it is never satisfying and there is always a desire for more.

According to the Bahá'í teachings, if we fulfil only our animal needs,
this leaves the other side of our nature, the human spirit, unfulfilled. Doing
so can never, therefore, be a path to contentment and happiness – that path
can only be found by developing and fulfilling our spiritual nature. To
become truly human involves trying to acquire gradually those qualities
that distinguish human beings from the animals.

TRUE FREEDOM

'Abdu'l-Bahá spent most of his early life a prisoner and an exile in the
company of his father, Bahá'u'lláh. When people said to 'Abdu'l-Bahá how
happy they were that he was now free, he replied:

Freedom is not a matter of place, but of condition. I was happy in that
prison, for those days were passed in the path of service.
To me prison was freedom.
Troubles are a rest to me.
Death is life.
To be despised is honour.
Therefore was I full of happiness all through that prison time.
When one is released from the prison of self, that indeed is freedom! For
self is the greatest prison.
When this release takes place, one can never be imprisoned. Unless one
accepts dire vicissitudes, not with dull resignation but with radiant
acquiescence, one cannot attain this freedom.

Words attributed to 'Abdu'l-Bahá in Blomfield,
The Chosen Highway, p. 166

PHYSICAL AND SPIRITUAL HEALTH

The Bahá'í teachings see human beings as being both physical and spiritual in nature. Health is therefore seen to be something that can only be achieved if there is well-being and balance in both the physical and the spiritual aspects of a person's life. We can achieve spiritual health by following the spiritual path described above. If we reach the stage indicated above, where we experience lasting contentment and joy, this clearly will also have a positive effect on our mental and physical health.

Indeed, one must look further than just the individual. For, as 'Abdu'l-Bahá has said, 'every part of the universe is connected with every other part by ties that are very powerful and admit of no imbalance, nor any slackening whatever'.[52] Therefore the interrelationships of individuals with those around them and with their environment will also affect their health – and, if this is not in balance, may cause disease. In this wider sense, many of the teachings of Bahá'u'lláh (such as the elimination of extremes of poverty, the advancement of women, universal education, see chapter 3) can be considered to be related to health.

Since human beings have both a physical and a spiritual aspect, illness can have both physical and spiritual causes and healing can be achieved by both physical and spiritual means:

There are two ways of healing sickness, material means and spiritual means. The first is by the treatment of physicians; the second consisteth in prayers offered by the spiritual ones to God and in turning to Him. Both means should be used and practised.

Illnesses which occur because of physical causes should be treated by doctors with medical remedies; those which are due to spiritual causes disappear through spiritual means. Thus an illness caused by affliction, fear, nervous impressions, will be healed more effectively by spiritual rather than by physical treatment. Hence, both kinds of treatment should be followed; they are not contradictory. Therefore thou shouldst also accept physical remedies inasmuch as these too have come from the mercy and favour of God, Who hath revealed and made manifest medical science so that His servants may profit from this kind of treatment also. Thou shouldst give equal attention to spiritual treatments, for they produce marvellous effects. ('Abdu'l-Bahá)[53]

Not all of the many aspects of the Bahá'í teachings on health can be explored here. Among the injunctions in the Bahá'í writings that have a bearing on health are:

- cleanliness
- a simple diet
- sexual chastity
- moderation in lifestyle
- abstaining from alcohol and mind-altering drugs, such as opium
- avoidance of smoking, which is regarded as unclean and damaging to health
- avoidance of anger, envy and jealousy

Although the Bahá'í scriptures advocate no particular diet, 'Abdu'l-Bahá has said that fruit, nuts and grains will eventually replace meat in the human diet.[54]

PRAYER FOR HEALING

Thy name is my healing, O my God, and remembrance of Thee is my remedy. Nearness to Thee is my hope, and love for Thee is my companion. Thy mercy to me is my healing and my succour in both this world and the world to come. Thou, verily, art the All-Bountiful, the All-Knowing, the All-Wise.

Bahá'u'lláh, *Prayers and Meditations*, no. 170, pp. 262–3

---

2 THE FAMILY

One way in which the world today differs most from previous ages is the breakdown of marriage and family life. In Europe and North America, each decade of the last half century has seen fewer people getting married and more of those who do marry later getting divorced. The family as the basic unit of society seems to be in danger of disappearing. Its place is being taken by a variety of social arrangements, in particular the one-parent family.

The Bahá'í teachings place great importance on the family both as the bedrock of the individual's spiritual development and as the foundation for society's stability and progress. This is because the family enables the raising and educating of children within a spiritual and harmonious environment. The subject of education is one that is given a great deal of importance in the Bahá'í Faith.

MARRIAGE

As with many other aspects of the Bahá'í Faith, marriage is seen as having both a physical and a spiritual aspect. 'Abdu'l-Bahá writes: 'Bahá'í marriage is the commitment of the two parties one to the other, and their mutual attachment of mind and heart.'[1] The spiritual aspects of this union are more important than the physical union.

> Marriage, among the mass of the people, is a physical bond, and this union can only be temporary, since it is foredoomed to a physical separation at the close.

Among the people of Bahá, however, marriage must be a union of the body and of the spirit as well, for here both husband and wife are aglow with the same wine, both are enamoured of the same matchless Face, both live and move through the same spirit, both are illumined by the same glory. This connection between them is a spiritual one, hence it is a bond that will abide forever. Likewise do they enjoy strong and lasting ties in the physical world as well, for if the marriage is based both on the spirit and the body, that union is a true one, hence it will endure. If, however, the bond is physical and nothing more, it is sure to be only temporary, and must inexorably end in separation. ('Abdu'l-Bahá)[2]

Similarly, Shoghi Effendi writes that although the sexual aspect of marriage is not unimportant, the spiritual side is more important:

Bahá'u'lláh has urged marriage upon all people as the natural and rightful way of life. He has also, however, placed strong emphasis on its spiritual nature, which, while in no way precluding a normal physical life, is the most essential aspect of marriage. That two people should live their lives in love and harmony is of far greater importance than that they should be consumed with passion for each other. The one is a great rock of strength on which to lean in time of need; the other a purely temporary thing which may at any time die out.[3]

'Abdu'l-Bahá says that if a couple succeed in achieving this state of spiritual harmony, then they will be happy in their married life, otherwise, problems will arise:

The Lord . . . hath made woman and man to abide with each other in the closest companionship, and to be even as a single soul. They are two helpmates, two intimate friends, who should be concerned about the welfare of each other.

If they live thus, they will pass through this world with perfect contentment, bliss, and peace of heart, and become the object of divine grace and favour in the Kingdom of heaven. But if they do other than this, they will live out their lives in great bitterness, longing at every moment for death, and will be shamefaced in the heavenly realm.

Strive, then, to abide, heart and soul, with each other as two doves in the nest, for this is to be blessed in both worlds.[4]

Couples are encouraged to 'exercise the utmost care to become thoroughly acquainted with the character of the other . . . Their purpose must be this: to become loving companions and comrades and at one with each other for time and eternity.'[5] The first goal in Bahá'í marriage is, therefore, to achieve a state of spiritual unity and companionship.

Separation and divorce, although permitted by Bahá'u'lláh, are nevertheless strongly discouraged: 'Truly, the Lord loveth union and harmony and abhorreth separation and divorce.'[6] The unity of the family is a foundational aspect of the unity of society that Bahá'u'lláh seeks to bring about. The Bahá'í scriptures, therefore, condemn divorce as a factor leading to social disintegration and a disruption of the family life necessary for the successful bringing up of children. It should therefore only be considered as 'a last resort'.[7] (For the Bahá'í laws regarding marriage and divorce, see pp. 88–9.)

CHILDREN AND FAMILY LIFE

The Bahá'í Faith teaches that if a husband and wife are truly united in a spiritual and physical marriage, then great results can come from that marriage. The most important of these is the raising of children:

> Thus the husband and wife are brought into affinity, are united and harmonized, even as though they were one person. Through their mutual union, companionship and love great results are produced in the world, both material and spiritual. The spiritual result is the appearance of divine bounties. The material result is the children who are born in the cradle of the love of God . . . Such children are those of whom it was said by Christ, 'Verily, they are the children of the Kingdom!'[8]

The first person to have extensive contact with a baby is usually the mother. While certain norms are acknowledged in the Bahá'í writings, such as the mother being 'the first educator of the child'[9] and the father having the responsibility to 'provide for and protect the family',[10] these are not intended to be applied inflexibly. It may occur in some families that the wife earns the family's income and the husband looks after the children. Responsibility for the education of children rests, however, with both parents. It is up to the couple to decide what is the best way to fulfil this responsibility. The seriousness of this responsibility may mean that other activities have to be sacrificed in order to perform this one well.

The Bahá'í teachings state that the most important task for the parents is to create an atmosphere of love and unity within the household. This is the atmosphere in which each individual, whether parent or child, can best develop her- or himself:

> Note ye how easily, where unity existeth in a given family, the affairs of that family are conducted; what progress the members of that family make, how they prosper in the world. Their concerns are in order, they enjoy comfort and tranquillity, they are secure, their position is assured, they come to be envied by all. Such a family but addeth to its stature and its lasting honour, as day succeedeth day. ('Abdu'l-Bahá)[11]

It is also of great importance that the parents themselves set the example for the conduct, morals and values that they are teaching the children, for children learn by example as much as or even more than through words. If parents want their children to be truthful, then they must be truthful; if they want their children to be free of racism (see pp. 34–7), then they must also be untainted by it; if they want their children to learn the equality of women and men (see pp. 37–40), then the husband and wife must show that quality in their dealings with each other.

The exact structure and composition of the family group is not prescribed in the Bahá'í writings. It may therefore consist of the 'nuclear family' or may include members of the 'extended family'. The emphasis in the Bahá'í teachings is on the processes and relationships within the family unit.

The relationships within the family should reflect what is regarded as the norm for relationships in the Bahá'í community which 'is not dictatorial authority, but humble fellowship, not arbitrary power, but the spirit of frank and loving consultation'.[12] The role of consultation is given great importance, both as a way of resolving conflicts that may arise between the marriage partners or between parents and children, and also as a social education for the children. (On Bahá'í consultation, see pp. 78–80).

Each person in the family must be respected as an individual and must be given both the love and the space to develop and grow:

> The integrity of the family bond must be constantly considered, and the rights of the individual members must not be transgressed. The rights of the son, the father, the mother – none of them must be transgressed, none of them must be arbitrary. Just as the son has certain obligations to his father, the father, likewise, has certain obligations to his son. The mother, the sister and other members of the household have their certain prerogatives. All these rights and prerogatives must be conserved, yet the unity of the family must be sustained. The injury of one shall be considered the injury of all; the comfort of each, the comfort of all; the honour of one, the honour of all.[13]

Similarly, violence towards, vilification or humilation of husband, wife or children are not an acceptable part of family life. 'Abdu'l-Bahá disapproved of the corporal punishment of children.

Children, for their part, are instructed to be respectful and obedient towards their parents and also to appreciate and be grateful for what has been done for them:

> Also a father and mother endure the greatest troubles and hardships for their children; and often when the children have reached the age of maturity, the parents pass on to the other world. Rarely does it happen that a father and mother in this world see the reward of the care and trouble they have undergone for their children. Therefore children, in return for this care and trouble, must show forth charity and beneficence, and must implore pardon and forgiveness for their parents.[14]

EDUCATION

Bahá'ís believe that the primary social function of marriage is to produce children and to train and educate them so that they become moral and spiritual human beings, individuals who will be spiritually content in themselves and useful members of society:

> The purport is this, that to train the character of humankind is one of the weightiest commandments of God, and the influence of such training is the same as that which the sun exerteth over tree and fruit. Children must be most carefully watched over, protected and trained; in such consisteth true parenthood and parental mercy.
>
> Otherwise, the children will turn into weeds growing wild . . . knowing not right from wrong, distinguishing not the highest of human qualities from all that is mean and vile; they will be brought up in vainglory . . .
>
> Wherefore doth every child, new-risen in the garden of Heavenly love, require the utmost training and care.[15]

So important is this task that Bahá'u'lláh raises it to the status of the worship of God: 'Know ye that in God's sight, the best of all ways to worship Him is to educate the children and train them in all the perfections of humankind; and no nobler deed than this can be imagined.'[16]

Education is, therefore, considered very important in the Bahá'í teachings. The basic function of education is outlined in the following quotation from Bahá'u'lláh: 'The Great Being saith: Regard man as a mine rich in gems of inestimable value. Education can, alone, cause it to reveal its treasures, and enable mankind to benefit therefrom.'[17]

THE IMPORTANCE OF EDUCATION

The root cause of wrongdoing is ignorance . . . Good character must be taught. Light must be spread afar, so that, in the school of humanity, all may acquire the heavenly characteristics of the spirit, and see for themselves beyond any doubt that there is no fiercer Hell, no more fiery abyss, than to possess a character that is evil and unsound . . .

The individual must be educated to such a high degree that he would rather have his throat cut than tell a lie . . . Thus will be kindled the sense of human dignity and pride . . .

It followeth that the children's school must be a place of utmost discipline and order, that instruction must be thorough, and provision must be made for the rectification and refinement of character; so that, in his earliest years, within the very essence of the child, the divine foundation will be laid and the structure of holiness raised up.

Know that this matter of instruction, of character rectification and refinement, of heartening and encouraging the child, is of the utmost importance, for such are basic principles of God . . .

It is extremely difficult to teach the individual and refine his character once puberty is passed. By then, as experience has shown, even if every effort be exerted to modify some tendency of his, it all availeth nothing. He may, perhaps, improve somewhat today; but let a few days pass and he forgetteth, and turneth backward to his habitual condition and accustomed ways. Therefore it is in early childhood that a firm foundation must be laid. While the branch is green and tender it can easily be made straight.

'Abdu'l-Bahá, *Selections*, no. 111, pp. 136–7

Each child can potentially therefore be of great benefit to humanity; it can also potentially be of great harm. The goal of educating children is to bring forth individuals who will improve the world through their character.

The education and training of children is among the most meritorious acts of humankind . . . for education is the indispensable foundation of all human excellence and alloweth man to work his way to the heights of abiding glory . . . For the inner reality of man is a demarcation line between the shadow and the light . . . Every child is potentially the light of the world – and at the same time its darkness; wherefore must the question of education be accounted as of primary importance. From his infancy, the child must be nursed at the breast of God's love, and nurtured in the embrace of His knowledge, that he may radiate light, grow in spirituality, be filled with wisdom and learning, and take on the characteristics of the angelic host. ('Abdu'l-Bahá)[18]

For these reasons, 'Abdu'l-Bahá says that if a mighty effort is exerted in the matter of education, the result will be a favourable transformation of the world of humanity.[19]

In many societies the idea has grown that the process of education is something that is the responsibility of schools. According to the Bahá'í teachings, however, the process of education begins from the moment of the birth of the child. In some senses, it begins even before this, for the Bahá'í writings include repeated statements about the importance of the education of girls because they will be the first educators of the next generation of children. Thus the mother (and the father) must prepare themselves for the education of their children even before the latter are born.

The earliest education of the child is received in the home and the earliest years are the most important: 'The babe, like unto a green and tender branch, will grow according to the way it is trained. If the training be right, it will grow right, and if crooked, the growth likewise, and unto the end of life it will conduct itself accordingly.'[20]

'Abdu'l-Bahá recommends that in the early years, children be taught prayers, and that emphasis be put on character and conduct.[21]

Let the mothers consider that whatever concerneth the education of children is of the first importance . . . Therefore is it incumbent upon the mothers to rear their little ones even as a gardener tendeth his young plants. Let them strive by day and by night to establish within their children faith and certitude . . . the love of the Beloved of the worlds, and all good qualities and traits. Whensoever a mother seeth that her child hath done well, let her praise and applaud him and cheer his heart; and if the slightest undesirable trait should manifest itself, let her counsel the child and punish him, and use means based on reason, even a slight verbal chastisement should this be necessary. It is not, however, permissible to strike a child, or vilify him, for the child's character will be totally perverted if he be subjected to blows or verbal abuse.[22]

After a few years, children must be sent to school, where they acquire the necessary knowledge to enable them to make a full contribution to society. 'Abdu'l-Bahá says that education is of three kinds. The first is physical education, which is concerned with enabling the individual to survive. The second is concerned with enabling the individual to partake of the fruits of human civilization, the arts, sciences, administration, etc. The third is spiritual education which causes the individual to acquire virtues and is thus necessary for that person to become a complete human being.[23] Unfortunately, in the world today, only the first two receive any attention in our schools. And yet the importance of the early years of education and schooling for the establishment of morality and order in society can scarcely be overstated. Because mothers are usually the first educators of the next generation, the schooling of girls is, according to the Bahá'í teachings, to be given priority over that of boys.[24]

◆

PRAYERS OF 'ABDU'L-BAHÁ FOR CHILDREN

O God! Educate these children. These children are the plants of Thine orchard, the flowers of Thy meadow, the roses of Thy garden. Let Thy rain fall upon them; let the Sun of Reality shine upon them with Thy love. Let Thy breeze refresh them in order that they may be trained, grow and develop, and appear in the utmost beauty. Thou art the Giver. Thou art the Compassionate.

Bahá'í Prayers, pp. 35–6

O my Lord! O my Lord!
   I am a child of tender years. Nourish me from the breast of Thy mercy, train me in the bosom of Thy love, educate me in the school of Thy guidance and develop me under the shadow of Thy bounty! Deliver me from darkness, make me a brilliant light; free me from unhappiness, make me a flower of the rose-garden; suffer me to become the servant of Thy Threshold and confer upon me the disposition and nature of the righteous ones; make me a cause of bounty to the human world, and crown my head with the diadem of eternal life!
   Verily, Thou art the Powerful, the Mighty, the Seer, the Hearer.

Bahá'í Prayers, pp. 37–8

◆

Once a firm moral and spiritual foundation has been laid in the character of the child, other subjects can be taught:

Arts, crafts and sciences uplift the world of being, and are conducive to its exaltation. Knowledge is as wings to man's life, and a ladder for his ascent. Its acquisition is incumbent upon everyone. The knowledge of such sciences, however, should be acquired as can profit the peoples of the earth. (Bahá'u'lláh)[25]

3 SOCIETY

As well as providing teachings for the spiritual welfare of the individual and of the family, Bahá'u'lláh has written a great deal on social matters. He has not given specific political and economic policies and laws; rather he has elaborated the underlying principles that must guide all social policies and laws if they are to be successful in bringing about the welfare and advancement of humanity.

Bahá'u'lláh identified unity, and the lack of it, in modern society as the principal matter that needs to be addressed by the peoples of the world. Few people need to be convinced of the fact that one of our major problems is the way in which social cohesiveness and the communal spirit have been undermined in the course of the twentieth century. Increasing numbers of people feel alienated from society. This may be because of their poverty, their lack of trust in those running society, their lack of the educational or intellectual capacity to deal with the complexities of modern society, or the prejudice against them because of their colour, ethnicity or religion. Each of these issues is addressed in the scriptures of the Bahá'í Faith (see also chapters 2 and 4).

A disunited and fragmented society is one in which little progress or development, either of the individual or of society as a whole, is possible. The energies of the society are consumed by its divisions and conflicts and by trying to resolve the problems caused thereby. Thus many of the teachings in the Bahá'í Faith revolve around this concept of unity and how to create it in society. (For more on the concept of unity itself, see chapter 4.)

FREEDOM FROM PREJUDICE

A major reason for the alienation of large numbers of people is the existence in society of deeply rooted prejudices. These prejudices are pernicious in that they are often built into the very structure of society in such a way that they cannot even be seen or recognized except by those who are adversely affected by them. They condemn many people in each society to being perpetual second-class citizens because they are women, black, poor, or belong to a certain ethnic, religious or caste grouping. As travel has brought diverse groups of people together and education has lifted their expectations of life, the problem of prejudice and alienation has become more acute.

The Bahá'í teachings strongly condemn the holding of prejudices of any kind. Bahá'u'lláh has emphasized the equality of all human beings:

> Know ye not why We created you all from the same dust? That no one should exalt himself over the other. Ponder at all times in your hearts how ye were created. Since We have created you all from one same substance it is incumbent on you to be even as one soul, to walk with the same feet, eat with the same mouth and dwell in the same land, that from your inmost being, by your deeds and actions, the signs of oneness and the essence of detachment may be made manifest.[1]

Specifically regarding prejudice and the disastrous effects of this upon human society, 'Abdu'l-Bahá has said: 'Prejudice – whether it be religious, racial, patriotic or political in its origin and aspect – is the destroyer of human foundations and opposed to the commands of God.'[2] This condemnation applies to prejudice of all forms. Thus for example religious prejudice is condemned:

> God has sent forth His Prophets for the sole purpose of creating love and unity in the world of human hearts. All the heavenly Books are the written word of love. If they prove to be the cause of prejudice and human estrangement, they have become fruitless. Therefore, religious prejudice is especially opposed to the will and command of God. ('Abdu'l-Bahá)[3]

Similarly, racial, ethnic and national prejudices are false. They are the product of artificial distinctions that human beings have erected to separate themselves from one another. Enormous amounts of energy and resources are wasted in keeping up these artificial barriers. In the twentieth century, nationalist and racist ideologies have led to two world wars, a host of minor conflicts, and devastation on the streets of our cities. The cost to humanity of these illusory ideas has been incalculable:

> Racial and national prejudices which separate mankind into groups and branches, likewise, have a false and unjustifiable foundation . . . There should be no racial alienation or national division among humankind. Such distinctions as French, German, Persian, Anglo-Saxon are human and artificial; they have neither significance nor recognition in the estimation of God. In His estimate all are one, the children of one family; and God is equally kind to them. The earth has one surface. God has not divided this surface by boundaries and barriers to separate races and peoples. Man has set up and established these imaginary lines, giving to each restricted area a name and the limitation of a native land or nationhood. By this division and separation into groups and branches of mankind, prejudice is engendered which becomes a fruitful source of war and strife . . . Therefore, it has been decreed by God in this day that these prejudices and differences shall be laid aside. ('Abdu'l-Bahá)[4]

◆

'ABDU'L-BAHÁ ON RACISM

In a talk given to a racially mixed audience in Chicago in 1912, 'Abdu'l-Bahá said:

In the human kingdom itself there are points of contact, properties common to all mankind; likewise, there are points of distinction which separate race from race, individual from individual. If the points of contact, which are the common properties of humanity, overcome the peculiar points of distinction, unity is assured. On the other hand, if the points of differentiation overcome the points of agreement, disunion and weakness result. One of the important questions which affect the unity and the solidarity of mankind is the fellowship and equality of the white and coloured races. Between these two races certain points of agreement and points of distinction exist which warrant just and mutual consideration. The points of contact are many; for in the material or physical plane of being, both are constituted alike and exist under the same law of growth and bodily development. Furthermore, both live and move in the plane of the senses and are endowed with human intelligence. There are many other mutual qualifications. In this country, the United States of America, patriotism is common to both races; all have equal rights to citizenship, speak one language, receive the blessings of the same civilization, and follow the precepts of the same religion. In fact numerous points of partnership and agreement exist between the two races; whereas the one point of distinction is that of colour. Shall this, the least of all distinctions, be allowed to separate you as races and individuals? In physical bodies, in the law of growth, in sense endowment, intelligence, patriotism, language, citizenship, civilization and religion you are one and the same. A single point of distinction exists – that of racial colour. God is not pleased with – neither should any reasonable or intelligent man be willing to recognize – inequality in the races because of this distinction.

But there is need of a superior power to overcome human prejudices, a power which nothing in the world of mankind can withstand and which will overshadow the effect of all other forces at work in human conditions. That irresistible power is the love of God. It is my hope and prayer that it may destroy the prejudice of this one point of distinction between you and unite you all permanently under its hallowed protection. Bahá'u'lláh has proclaimed the oneness of the world of humanity. He has caused various nations and divergent creeds to unite. He has declared that difference of race and colour is like the variegated beauty of flowers in a garden . . . If all the flowers in a garden were of the same colour, the effect would be monotonous and wearying to the eye.

Therefore, Bahá'u'lláh hath said that the various races of humankind lend a composite harmony and beauty of colour to the whole. Let all associate, therefore, in this great human garden even as flowers grow and blend together side by side without discord or disagreement between them.

Promulgation of Universal Peace, pp. 67–9

◆

THE ADVANCEMENT OF WOMEN

In modern societies, the largest group suffering from the effects of prejudice is often women. For most of recorded history and in most of the world, human society has been a patriarchy – dominated by men. The very structures of these societies have made it difficult for women to achieve their full potential or to have any effective say in the ordering of society. In a sense then, the position of women is one aspect of the discussion in the previous section about prejudice in society. Since women form such a large part of every society, however, the subject has received special attention in the teachings of the Bahá'í Faith.

Bahá'u'lláh asserted, in several places in his writings, that men and women have an equal rank and station before God:

Exalted, immensely exalted is He Who hath removed differences and established harmony. Glorified, infinitely glorified is He Who hath caused discord to cease, and decreed solidarity and unity. Praised be God, the Pen of the Most High hath lifted distinctions from between His servants and

handmaidens, and, through His consummate favours and all-encom-
passing mercy, hath conferred upon all a station and rank of the same
plane. He hath broken the back of vain imaginings with the sword of
utterance and hath obliterated the perils of idle fancies through the
pervasive power of His might.[5]

◆

THE EQUALITY OF WOMEN AND MEN

In past ages it was held that woman and man were not equal – that is to say,
woman was considered inferior to man, even from the standpoint of her
anatomy and creation. She was considered especially inferior in
intelligence, and the idea prevailed universally that it was not allowable for
her to step into the arena of important affairs. In some countries man went so
far as to believe and teach that woman belonged to a sphere lower than
human. But in this century, which is the century of light and the revelation of
mysteries, God is proving to the satisfaction of humanity that all this is
ignorance and error; nay, rather, it is well established that mankind and
womankind as parts of composite humanity are coequal and that no
difference in estimate is allowable, for all are human . . . In reality, God has
created all mankind, and in the estimation of God there is no distinction as to
male and female. The one whose heart is pure is acceptable in His sight, be
that one man or woman. God does not inquire, 'Art thou woman or art thou
man?' He judges human actions. If these are acceptable in the threshold of
the Glorious One, man and woman will be equally recognized and rewarded.

'Abdu'l-Bahá, *Promulgation of Universal Peace*, p. 133

◆

Nor are women inferior to men in their abilities; any deficiency shown in
the past was solely due to a lack of education and opportunities:

It has been objected by some that woman is not equally capable with man
and that she is deficient by creation. This is pure imagination. The
difference in capability between man and woman is due entirely to
opportunity and education. Heretofore woman has been denied the right
and privilege of equal development. If equal opportunity be granted her,
there is no doubt she would be the peer of man . . .

The purpose, in brief, is this: that if woman be fully educated and granted
her rights, she will attain the capacity for wonderful accomplishments and
prove herself the equal of man. She is the coadjutor of man, his complement
and helpmeet. Both are human; both are endowed with potentialities of
intelligence and embody the virtues of humanity. In all human powers and

functions they are partners and coequals. At present in spheres of human activity woman does not manifest her natal prerogatives, owing to lack of education and opportunity. Without doubt education will establish her equality with men. ('Abdu'l-Bahá)[6]

In some respects, 'Abdu'l-Bahá asserts, the woman is 'of the greater importance to the race. She has the greater burden and the greater work . . . The woman has greater moral courage than the man; she has also special gifts which enable her to govern in moments of danger and crisis.'[7] She is also 'more tender-hearted, more receptive, her intuition is more intense'.[8]

'Abdu'l-Bahá says that this teaching of the equality of women and men is an important one for the progress of humanity:

And among the teachings of Bahá'u'lláh is the equality of women and men. The world of humanity has two wings – one is women and the other men. Not until both wings are equally developed can the bird fly. Should one wing remain weak, flight is impossible. Not until the world of women becomes equal to the world of men in the acquisition of virtues and perfections, can success and prosperity be attained as they ought to be.[9]

And so therefore: 'As long as women are prevented from attaining their highest possibilities, so long will men be unable to achieve the greatness which might be theirs.'[10] In particular, 'Abdu'l-Bahá asserts that an increased role for women in society is necessary for the achievement of world peace.

As well as affirming the equality of men and women, the Bahá'í teachings recognize the necessity of dismantling some of the social structures that maintain patriarchal society. These features of the Bahá'í social order, such as the removal of authority from individuals and the decentralization of power, will be discussed in a later chapter (see chapter 5). In all, the aim is to achieve a better balance in society between its masculine and feminine elements:

The world in the past has been ruled by force, and man has dominated over woman by reason of his more forceful and aggressive qualities both of body and mind. But the balance is already shifting; force is losing its dominance, and mental alertness, intuition, and the spiritual qualities of love and service, in which woman is strong, are gaining ascendancy. Hence the new age will be an age less masculine and more permeated with the feminine ideals, or, to speak more exactly, will be an age in which the masculine and feminine elements of civilization will be more evenly balanced. ('Abdu'l-Bahá)[11]

Although women are guaranteed full equality with men, there is some inevitable complementarity in their social roles. Women are free to follow any occupation that they wish, but it is envisaged that they will be the first educators of any children that are born to them. As stated in the previous chapter, because of the importance of their role as the first educators of children, the Bahá'í Faith teaches that, if there is any difficulty in the full provision of education, preference should be given to girls over boys. Women are, however, precluded from membership of the Universal House of Justice (see p. 70). 'Abdu'l-Bahá says that this is 'for a wisdom of the Lord God's, which will ere long be made manifest as clearly as the sun at high noon.'[12] Bahá'ís must take this apparent anomaly as a matter of faith for the present.

SCIENCE, TECHNOLOGY AND THE ENVIRONMENT

The Bahá'í worldview accords the sciences and technology a high place. The human mind and its reasoning ability are one of the distinguishing marks of humanity, and science, which is one of the fruits of this, is regarded as a divine gift. In particular, the conflict that has occurred between science and religion over such concepts as evolution is considered to have been wrong. Science and religion should instead be seen as complementary aspects of human progress and development. 'Abdu'l-Bahá says:

> Religion and science are the two wings upon which man's intelligence can soar into the heights, with which the human soul can progress. It is not possible to fly with one wing alone! Should a man try to fly with the wing of religion alone he would quickly fall into the quagmire of superstition, whilst on the other hand, with the wing of science alone he would also make no progress, but fall into the despairing slough of materialism.[13]

Human beings, through the instrument of science and technology, have achieved a mastery over nature. Without religion, however, that mastery can become disastrous; science and technology can become the instruments of warfare or lead to environmental pollution. Bahá'u'lláh warned of the dangers of the excesses of our civilization:

> The civilization, so often vaunted by the learned exponents of arts and sciences, will, if allowed to overleap the bounds of moderation, bring

great evil upon men. Thus warneth you He Who is the All-Knowing. If
carried to excess, civilization will prove as prolific a source of evil as it
had been of goodness when kept within the restraints of moderation.
Meditate on this, O people, and be not of them that wander distraught in
the wilderness of error. The day is approaching when its flame will devour
the cities.[14]

Humanity's arrogant misuse of nature has led to a situation where
environmental calamities threaten in many different ways. Humanity
must learn to overcome this arrogance and adopt a more humble
approach towards the earth and what it contains.

Every man of discernment, while walking upon the earth, feeleth indeed
abashed, inasmuch as he is fully aware that the thing which is the source
of his prosperity, his wealth, his might, his exaltation, his advancement
and power is, as ordained by God, the very earth which is trodden
beneath the feet of all men. There can be no doubt that whoever is
cognizant of this truth, is cleansed and sanctified from all pride,
arrogance, and vainglory. (Bahá'u'lláh)[15]

Indeed, contemplating nature can be a way of contemplating the
Divine:

When, however, thou dost contemplate the innermost essence of all
things, and the individuality of each, thou wilt behold the signs of thy
Lord's mercy in every created thing, and see the spreading rays of His
Names and Attributes throughout all the realm of being . . . And
whensoever thou dost gaze upon creation all entire, and dost observe the
very atoms thereof, thou wilt note that the rays of the Sun of Truth are
shed upon all things and shining within them, and telling of that Day-
Star's splendours, Its mysteries, and the spreading of Its lights. Look thou
upon the trees, upon the blossoms and fruits, even upon the stones. Here
too wilt thou behold the Sun's rays shed upon them, clearly visible within
them, and manifested by them. ('Abdu'l-Bahá)[16]

And from this contemplation of nature, we come to recognize the
interconnectedness of all things and the necessity of taking care of our
environment:

We cannot segregate the human heart from the environment outside us
and say that once one of these is reformed everything will be improved.
Man is organic with the world. His inner life moulds the environment and
is itself also deeply affected by it. The one acts upon the other and every

abiding change in the life of man is the result of these mutual reactions. (Shoghi Effendi)[17]

LIBERTY AND HUMAN RIGHTS

All around us there are many individuals and groups claiming rights and freedoms. The desire and drive for freedom has been one of the main themes of the twentieth century. Religious freedom, political freedom, the right to free speech, the right to work freely, the right to spend your money freely, the freedom to travel; all of these are freedoms that have gradually been won, in the West at least, during this century. The question must however be raised as to where this quest for freedom stops.

Individualism, the cult of the individual, has reached such a high level in the West that society is now contemplating its adverse effects. Is the individual to be given the freedom to do whatever he or she likes? Is the freedom to carry any type of weapon, the licence to undertake all types of sexual activities, or the liberty to publish or broadcast any type of attack on a minority group also going to be allowed? Another question that arises is whether these freedoms that have been gained have really led to a greater degree of human happiness. No one can deny or fail to be grateful for the fact that there has been great progress in freeing millions of human beings from tyrannical oppression by governments, religious authorities and other powerful institutions. But there has simultaneously been an increasing sense of isolation and dislocation for individuals in society.

As the century has progressed, the cult of individualism has gained in strength and become a central feature of Western society. We have reached the point where the central preoccupation of most politicians and social commentators appears to be the devising of strategies to give individuals more and more rights and freedoms. The libertarian doctrines of the political left insist on the right of the individual to pursue self-fulfilment. The free-market capitalism of the political right insists on the freedom to maximize profit and the rights of the individual as consumer. Both sides of the political spectrum have thus fuelled the trend of the past few decades leading to the growth of individualism.

The effect of all of this on the community has only recently been recognized. To give people greater and greater freedom without balancing this with a greater sense of responsibility in their use of that freedom leads to a society in which people are pursuing their own desires and indulging themselves whatever the effect this might have on others. This freedom and self-indulgence finds expression in drug abuse, alcoholism, vandalism, violence, sexual promiscuity and a general lack of respect for the rights and dignity of others. It leads in turn to crime on the part of those who cannot legitimately earn the money to be a part of the consumer society; to depression, suicide and drug dependence in those who are the victims of the culture of greed and the social isolation that is created; and to corruption among the rich and powerful.

The group that has perhaps been most affected by this most is children. The educational practices of the past, which included trying to instil a sense of self-discipline and social responsibility into children, have been widely discarded, and replaced by practices based on the theory that children should be given the greatest amount of freedom possible to develop themselves. The extent to which this has been carried has left many children without a structure or framework to their lives. When confronted with a society that itself has lost its standards and its sense of moderation, these children often have neither the maturity to deal with the freedom that is thrust upon them by society nor the social support of a caring adult society upon which to fall back.

Over a century ago, Bahá'u'lláh gave much the same analysis of the social situation and the direction in which it was heading. He rejected the idea that unlimited freedom is beneficial to human beings. Liberty, he asserted, if carried to excess, is as great a source of evil as a moderate degree of it is a source of good:

> We find some men desiring liberty, and priding themselves therein. Such men are in the depths of ignorance ... Know ye that the embodiment of liberty and its symbol is the animal. That which beseemeth man is submission unto such restraints as will protect him from his own ignorance, and guard him against the harm of the mischief-maker. Liberty causeth man to overstep the bounds of propriety, and to infringe on the dignity of his station. It debaseth him to the level of extreme depravity and wickedness ... We approve of liberty in certain circumstances, and refuse to sanction it in others.[18]

Bahá'u'lláh expounds a principle in relationship to liberty that has a much wider application – the principle of moderation. He says that however much something may appear to be good, if it is carried to excess it becomes a source of evil:

> It is incumbent upon them who are in authority to exercise moderation in all things. Whatsoever passeth beyond the limits of moderation will cease to exert a beneficial influence. Consider for instance such things as liberty, civilization and the like. However much men of understanding may favourably regard them, they will, if carried to excess, exercise a pernicious influence upon men.[19]

Human rights must stem from a knowledge of the dignity and worth of every individual human being – a knowledge that is enshrined in the scriptures of most religions. ʻAbduʼl-Bahá says that the teachings of Baháʼuʼlláh

> are addressed to humanity. He says, 'Ye are all the leaves of one tree' . . . Even though we find a defective branch or leaf upon this tree of humanity or an imperfect blossom, it, nevertheless, belongs to this tree and not to another. Therefore, it is our duty to protect and cultivate this tree until it reaches perfection. If we examine its fruit and find it imperfect, we must strive to make it perfect. There are souls in the human world who are ignorant; we must make them knowing. Some growing upon the tree are weak and ailing; we must assist them toward health and recovery. If they are as infants in development, we must minister to them until they attain maturity. We should never detest and shun them as objectionable and unworthy. We must treat them with honour, respect and kindness . . . In brief, all humanity must be looked upon with love, kindness and respect.[20]

ʻAbduʼl-Bahá has stated that society must adopt equal and guaranteed human rights for all: 'Baháʼuʼlláh taught that an equal standard of human rights must be recognized and adopted. In the estimation of God all men are equal; there is no distinction or preferment for any soul in the dominion of His justice and equity.'[21]

The above should not be read as implying that the Baháʼí teachings condemn freedom and liberty. On the contrary, they advocate that increased liberty and human rights based on justice are important advances which allow individuals the opportunity to develop their full human potential. Baháʼuʼlláh warns, however, that this trend should not be allowed to proceed to the extreme point where it threatens the order and stability of society.

AGRICULTURE

In most countries that have become industrialized and have advanced materially, the importance of agriculture has decreased. 'Abdu'l-Bahá says, however, that it is 'the fundamental basis of the community'[22] and that 'the peasant class and the agricultural class exceed other classes in the importance of their service'.[23] Bahá'u'lláh asserts that 'special regard must be paid to agriculture' as it is an activity that is 'conducive to the advancement of mankind and to the reconstruction of the world'.[24]

'Abdu'l-Bahá has outlined a scheme that would make rural communities more self-sufficient and less vulnerable to natural disasters. He suggested the accumulation of a public treasury in each rural community, which would relieve suffering in the case of the poor, the incapacitated and those suffering as a result of misfortunes or natural disasters, and thus make these communities more independent.[25]

TEACHINGS ON GOVERNMENT AND SOCIAL POLICY

Bahá'u'lláh addressed the kings and rulers of his time on a number of issues, many of which continue to have relevance today. Surveying the world of his time, he noted that there were two main models of government, the authoritarian, absolutist model represented by the Tsar of Russia, the Sultan of Ottoman Turkey or the Shah of Iran, and the democratic model, which was especially associated with the new republic formed in the United States of America and with Britain. He strongly advocated the democratic model. He recommended, however, that a monarch be kept as head of state since 'the majesty of kingship is one of the signs of God. We do not wish that the countries of the world should remain deprived thereof.'[26] He therefore advised a combination of democracy and kingship (i.e. a constitutional monarchy).

Bahá'u'lláh particularly admonished the rulers and governments of the world to establish peace and to reduce unnecessary expenditure on armaments:

Compose your differences, and reduce your armaments, that the burden of your expenditures may be lightened, and that your minds and hearts may be tranquillized. Heal the dissensions that divide you, and ye will no longer be in need of any armaments except what the protection of your cities and territories demandeth. Fear ye God, and take heed not to outstrip the bounds of moderation, and be numbered among the extravagant.

We have learned that you are increasing your outlay every year, and are laying the burden thereof on your subjects. This, verily, is more than they can bear, and is a grievous injustice.[27]

One quality that Bahá'u'lláh particularly commends to those in authority is justice:

Be vigilant, that ye may not do injustice to anyone, be it to the extent of a grain of mustard seed. Tread ye the path of justice, for this, verily, is the straight path . . . Decide justly between men, and be ye the emblems of justice amongst them . . . Beware not to deal unjustly with any one that appealeth to you, and entereth beneath your shadow . . .

Know ye that the poor are the trust of God in your midst. Watch that ye betray not His trust, that ye deal not unjustly with them and that ye walk not in the ways of the treacherous . . .

God hath committed into your hands the reins of the government of the people, that ye may rule with justice over them, safeguard the rights of the down-trodden, and punish the wrong-doers. If ye neglect the duty prescribed unto you by God in His Book, your names shall be numbered with those of the unjust in His sight.[28]

Bahá'u'lláh also addressed the elected representatives of the people urging them to maintain the highest moral standards: 'O ye the elected representatives of the people in every land! Take ye counsel together, and let your concern be only for that which profiteth mankind, and bettereth the condition thereof.'[29]

Among those matters in which the utmost probity should be exercised is the appointment and promotion of officials. These appointments must be made according to fitness and merit and not because of family or personal connections:

Governments should fully acquaint themselves with the conditions of those they govern, and confer upon them positions according to desert and merit. It is enjoined upon every ruler and sovereign to consider this matter with the utmost care that the traitor may not usurp the position of the faithful, nor the despoiler rule in the place of the trustworthy. (Bahá'u'lláh)[30]

'Abdu'l-Bahá wrote a book, *The Secret of Divine Civilization*, much of which deals with the qualities necessary for government leaders and officials.

The question of how decisions are made in society is an important one. At present, decision making tends to be the prerogative of an individual leader or a small group in power. In the Bahá'í teachings, great importance is attached to group decision making by a consultative process. Bahá'ís consider the development of the skill of effective consultation to be an important part of social and community development. The process of consultation, however, is one which, in the Bahá'í view, is very underdeveloped at present. (On the underlying principles of Bahá'í consultation, see pp. 78–80.)

Crime and its punishment is a social issue that concerns many people. On the subject of the treatment of criminals, 'Abdu'l-Bahá says that the individual does not have the right to exact vengeance. The community as a whole, however, needs to protect its members from harm:

> If someone oppresses, injures and wrongs another, and the wronged man retaliates, this is vengeance and is censurable . . . But the community has the right of defense and of self-protection; moreover, the community has no hatred nor animosity for the murderer: it imprisons or punishes him merely for the protection and security of others. It is not for the purpose of taking vengeance upon the murderer, but for the purpose of inflicting a punishment by which the community will be protected. If the community and the inheritors of the murdered one were to forgive and return good for evil, the cruel would be continually ill-treating others, and assassinations would continually occur . . . The tent of existence is upheld upon the pillar of justice and not upon forgiveness. The continuance of mankind depends upon justice and not upon forgiveness.[31]

Alongside this administration of justice, however, 'Abdu'l-Bahá also advocates that our eventual aim must be to educate children so as to make the committing of a crime itself a rare thing in society:

> But the most essential thing is that the people must be educated in such a way that no crimes will be committed; for it is possible to educate the masses so effectively that they will avoid and shrink from perpetrating

crimes, so that the crime itself will appear to them as the greatest chastisement, the utmost condemnation and torment. Therefore, no crimes which require punishment will be committed.

. . . Communities are day and night occupied in making penal laws, and in preparing and organizing instruments and means of punishment. They build prisons, make chains and fetters, arrange places of exile and banishment, and different kinds of hardships and tortures, and think by these means to discipline criminals, whereas, in reality, they are causing destruction of morals and perversion of characters. The community, on the contrary, ought day and night to strive and endeavour with the utmost zeal and effort to accomplish the education of men, to cause them day by day to progress and to increase in science and knowledge, to acquire virtues, to gain good morals and to avoid vices, so that crimes may not occur.[32]

TEACHINGS ON ECONOMICS

The Bahá'í texts also contain passages dealing with economic matters. One of the main ways in which people, especially politicians, think that they will be able to solve the problems that our societies face is through economic manipulation. Various economic theories are propounded, but the inevitable experience is that when those who advocate these theories come to power, the measures that they enact do not bring about the anticipated benefits. According to the Bahá'í teachings, much of the economic activity in the world today is wrongly conceived because it is built upon incorrect assumptions.

The first of these incorrect assumptions is the idea that human happiness and contentment can be achieved merely by increasing the wealth of the individual members of the society. Economists assume that all human beings are motivated by selfishness and greed and that therefore the more any particular economic policy caters for these base motivations, the more successful it will be. And so most economic theories are put forward on the basis that they will give increased wealth to the members of the society. According to the Bahá'í teachings, that is not the right way to achieve human happiness and contentment – human beings will only be satisfied if the spiritual aspect of their nature is fulfilled and developed alongside the physical (see chapter 1).

The second incorrect assumption is that it is possible to achieve lasting benefits for one section of society or one part of the world at the expense of other sections or parts of the world. This again is a false concept according to the Bahá'í teachings. It may be that a particular policy will bring temporary benefits to one social class or one country at the expense of other classes or other countries, but that is only a temporary gain, and the policy is short sighted. Because of the interconnectedness of all humanity, if any part of humanity is adversely affected by the policy, then in the long run all of humanity will be adversely affected. We must cease to regard ourselves as belonging to particular factions or races or nations of humankind and we must start to regard humanity as one people and the whole world as one country. Only an economic policy that benefits all will in the long run benefit anyone.

The third incorrect assumption made by economists when formulating their theories, and this one is perhaps the most important of all, is the idea that materialistic economic theories can actually solve economic problems. 'Abdu'l-Bahá says that economic problems are at their deepest level spiritual in nature and so they can only be solved by correcting the underlying spiritual problems – problems such as injustice, corruption and selfishness. The solution to the economic ills of the world, therefore, according to the Bahá'í teachings, lies not in applying elaborate and sophisticated economic theories or even in legislation or political manipulations. The underlying cause of these economic problems is a spiritual malaise that affects the whole world and so only a spiritual solution will cure these economic problems:

> The fundamentals of the whole economic condition are divine in nature and are associated with the world of the heart and spirit . . . Strive, therefore, to create love in the hearts in order that they may become glowing and radiant. When that love is shining, it will permeate other hearts even as this electric light illumines its surroundings. When the love of God is established, everything else will be realized. This is the true foundation of all economics . . . Economic questions are most interesting; but the power which moves, controls and attracts the hearts of men is the love of God. ('Abdu'l-Bahá)[33]

It is, therefore, not surprising to find that the Bahá'í Faith does not advocate any particular existing economic theory, nor does it add a new one. One of the principal concepts in the Bahá'í Faith is the idea that the social structure of humanity is constantly changing and so no economic theory is always going to be right for the whole world. Instead, in the

Bahá'í scriptures, a number of principles are put forward which must be the basis for any specific economic plans. These economic principles include:

- **The need for world peace** As mentioned above, at present the economies of so many countries are crippled by the expenditure necessary to purchase large quantities of arms. Even very poor nations that barely have enough to feed themselves are spending a large proportion of their national incomes on armaments. A necessary precursor for the solution of the world's economic problems, then, is the establishment of world peace and a collective security arrangement that will enable all countries to reduce their expenditure on arms (see pp. 60–1).

- **The need for a world economy** As has already been pointed out, we must take the benefit of the whole of humanity into consideration when planning economic measures and so all economic planning must be done inside a global perspective. When each measure is planned, the following question must be asked: 'Is this measure going to be of overall benefit to the whole of humanity?' The resources of the planet would then be developed for the benefit of all and not for the profit of a few. Part of the development of a global economy will be the need to move towards a world currency, a world system of weights and measures, and international regulation of the terms of trade.

- **The need for justice in the economic system** One of the key spiritual qualities that should govern all public affairs is justice. In economic terms this means that one section of society should not be able to maintain control over all the means of production and distribution in a society and thus maintain an economic stranglehold on that society so that this elite becomes very rich while everyone else is condemned to poverty. Such imbalances and injustice exist both within countries and between countries. Some countries have great wealth and waste enormous resources of energy and materials; and these countries have policies that are instrumental in keeping other countries very poor, to the extent that some do not have enough even to feed their populations. Part of the problem is the unfair terms of trade between the rich countries and the poor countries, and this must be addressed at the global level. Another part of the problem is the consumerism and excessive competition in the richer countries which leads to enormous waste and exorbitant consumption. At the level of the individual, the Bahá'í teachings suggest that such measures as a progressive income tax will eliminate the extremes of wealth and poverty in a society. It is important to note that the Bahá'í Faith does not claim that we either can or should try to achieve complete equality of wealth among all people or the forced redistribution of wealth, as is advocated by some versions of socialist doctrine. It is an illusion to believe that it is ever possible to reach such a state. Human beings are varied in their intelligence and abilities, and one can never achieve a complete equalization of wealth. In addition, under Bahá'í law, everyone is entitled to own property and to pass on that property to whoever they wish. What Bahá'ís are advocating is that extremes of poverty and wealth should be eliminated.

- **A new work ethic** Bahá'u'lláh says that in this age it is possible and necessary for the world to arrange its affairs in such a way that all people receive an education and also receive training so that they are able to work and earn their livelihood. And it is also an obligation placed on each individual that they perform some useful work in society. Bahá'u'lláh even introduces a new work ethic when he says that work performed conscientiously and in the spirit of service to humanity is equivalent to the worship of God (see pp. 19–20).

- **The importance of co-operation** At present much of the economic scene is dominated by competition and conflict. Although a small degree of competition is useful, today in many parts of the world, it has reached a stage of being wasteful and destructive. There should be an increased emphasis on co-operation in society. This can only be achieved, however, if individuals stop being self-centred and look instead to what will benefit society as a whole. In particular 'Abdu'l-Bahá states that in industry, we must move away from the present situation of conflict between the workers and the owners of an enterprise, which results in strikes and wastefulness. He says that the owners of an enterprise should share some of the profits of the enterprise with the workers, so that the workers receive their wages and a share of the profits of the company. This removes the conflict of interest between the workers and the owners, and encourages both sides to work in co-operation.[34]

- **The importance of voluntary sharing** Bahá'u'lláh places great importance upon the virtues and benefits of voluntary sharing. It will be a sign of the spiritualization of society when the rich realize that their wealth is a spiritual hindrance to them and voluntarily share with the poor.

VOLUNTARY SHARING

The Teachings of Bahá'u'lláh advocate voluntary sharing, and this is a greater thing than the equalization of wealth. For equalization must be imposed from without, while sharing is a matter of free choice.

Man reacheth perfection through good deeds, voluntarily performed, not through good deeds the doing of which was forced upon him. And sharing is a personally chosen righteous act: that is, the rich should extend assistance to the poor, they should expend their substance for the poor, but of their own free will, and not because the poor have gained this end by force. For the harvest of force is turmoil and the ruin of the social order. On the other hand voluntary sharing, the freely-chosen expending of one's substance, leadeth to society's comfort and peace. It lighteth up the world; it bestoweth honour upon humankind.

'Abdu'l-Bahá, *Selections*, p. 115

It is important to note that these are just general guiding principles. The Bahá'í teachings assert, however, that the sickness of society cannot be cured by economic policies or by laws. The sickness is a spiritual sickness and as long as the individual members of society are greedy, selfish, materialistic and prejudiced, there can be no long-term solution. These spiritual ills need a spiritual cure. Only religious faith has the power to transform people and thus cure this spiritual disease. Only when the individuals in a society are spiritually transformed is there any hope of a lasting cure to the social, political and economic problems.

GENERAL PRINCIPLES AND OTHER TEACHINGS

It can be observed that rather than having a specific programme of social laws that it aims to put into place, the Bahá'í Faith has general social principles that serve to guide social policy. In the Bahá'í view the advancement of human civilization must happen gradually and organically. It does not occur through political leadership or legislation. It can only occur through individuals who are motivated to transform their own lives and, in so doing, gradually transform society.

The Bahá'í social teachings are thus phrased in terms of the general spiritual principles, such as equality and justice, that must underlie any social change. Many other social teachings can be found in the Bahá'í writings. Most of these are based either on the underlying spiritual principle of justice or they promote a global vision and a truly integrated world order. Among these is the injunction for the governments of the world to adopt a universal language to be taught in all schools alongside the mother tongue of each nation; the adoption of a universal system of weights and measures; the adoption of a universal standard of human rights; and the universal compulsory education of children.

4 GLOBAL CONCERNS

Bahá'u'lláh's teachings are concerned not just with issues within a particular society but also with global issues. Indeed, the Bahá'í teachings maintain that many of the problems that afflict us at present can only be solved if they are tackled at the global level.

THE UNITY OF HUMANKIND

Humanity has evolved through various stages of ever greater social groupings: tribal societies, various feudal systems, city-states, and the nation-state. Each stage of this evolution has, as it has developed, thrown up problems that have only been resolved when humanity has moved on to the next stage of its evolution. Our present world situation has resulted from the emergence of the modern nation-state. This stage of human evolution has now developed political, economic, ecological and other pressing problems that are in urgent need of solutions. Bahá'u'lláh says that humanity must now evolve beyond this stage to that of global unity.

In some of his writings, Bahá'u'lláh calls himself the Divine Physician called to diagnose and treat the illness of the world. He says that his diagnosis of the disease afflicting humanity is its disunity. Only by establishing unity can there be peace and prosperity, and only the teachings that he has brought can establish this unity: 'The well-being of mankind, its peace and security, are unattainable unless and until its unity is firmly established. This unity can never be achieved so long as the counsels which the Pen of the Most High hath revealed are suffered to pass unheeded.'[1] Bahá'u'lláh calls on all human beings to set their faces towards unity and to allow its powerful healing effects to cure the ills of society: 'Deal ye one with another with the utmost love and harmony, with friendliness and fellowship. He Who is the Day-Star of Truth beareth Me witness! So powerful is the light of unity that it can illuminate the whole earth.'[2]

This coming together of people in unity and harmony is, Bahá'u'lláh asserts, the fundamental purpose of religion: 'The fundamental purpose animating the Faith of God and His Religion is to safeguard the interests and promote the unity of the human race, and to foster the spirit of love and fellowship amongst men.'[3]

The application of this principle of unity would see far-reaching changes in many aspects of community life. Adversarial principles govern many of our social institutions: politics, the courts, business, and even many professional and social activities; and to an even greater extent the running of international affairs. When statesmen come together in international bodies such as the United Nations, it is almost axiomatic that the only concern of each will be what is best for their own country regardless of what effect this may have on the rest of the world. Bahá'u'lláh asserts that this combative approach is undesirable; society should be regarded as an organism, such as the human body. The organs of the body are different from each other, and yet, for the body to function effectively, the various parts need to work in unity and harmony.[4]

Many people have misgivings about greater degrees of social unity and integration, fearing the dictatorial power envisaged in George Orwell's novel *1984*. In fact, however, history shows that greater degrees of social unity have led to increasing freedom for individuals to develop their potential and increased safeguards of human rights against oppressive measures taken by those in authority. Thus, for example, the present moves towards European unity give the individual citizen greater rights and freedoms than before: the right to take his or her own government to the European Court of Human Rights, for example.

Bahá'u'lláh sees this coming together of the peoples of the world as an inevitable occurrence. Most of the problems that the world faces (including environmental pollution, desertification, global warming, and the gap between rich and poor nations) are only soluble if they are dealt with at a global level. These problems will therefore continue to get worse until the world wakes up to this fact:

> Behold the disturbances which, for many a long year, have afflicted the
> earth, and the perturbation that hath seized its peoples. It hath either been
> ravaged by war, or tormented by sudden and unforeseen calamities.
> Though the world is encompassed with misery and distress, yet no man
> hath paused to reflect what the cause or source of that may be. Whenever
> the True Counsellor uttered a word in admonishment, lo, they all
> denounced Him as a mover of mischief and rejected His claim . . . The
> evidences of discord and malice are apparent everywhere, though all were
> made for harmony and union. The Great Being saith: O well-beloved
> ones! The tabernacle of unity hath been raised; regard ye not one another
> as strangers. Ye are the fruits of one tree, and the leaves of one branch.
> (Bahá'u'lláh)[5]

◆

THE NEED FOR A GLOBAL CONSCIOUSNESS

In October 1911, Italian forces landed in Tripoli and Benghazi, thus occupying
the last part of North Africa that was still part of the Ottoman Turkish Empire.
(This event signalled the culmination of the European colonization of Africa.)
One day in November 1911 in Paris, 'Abdu'l-Bahá said:

I have just been told that there has been a terrible accident in this country. A
train has fallen into the river and at least twenty people have been killed. This
is going to be a matter for discussion in the French Parliament today, and the
Director of the State Railway will be called upon to speak. He will be cross-
examined as to the condition of the railroad and as to what caused the
accident, and there will be a heated argument. I am filled with wonder and
surprise to notice what interest and excitement has been aroused throughout
the whole country on account of the death of twenty people, while they remain
cold and indifferent to the fact that thousands of Italians, Turks, and Arabs are
killed in Tripoli! The horror of this wholesale slaughter has not disturbed the
Government at all! Yet these unfortunate people are human beings too.

Why is there so much interest and eager sympathy shown towards these
twenty individuals, while for five thousand persons there is none? They are all
men, they all belong to the family of mankind, but they are of other lands and
races. It is no concern of the disinterested countries if these men are cut to
pieces, this wholesale slaughter does not affect them! How unjust, how cruel
is this, how utterly devoid of any good and true feeling! The people of these
other lands have children and wives, mothers, daughters, and little sons! In
these countries today there is hardly a house free from the sound of bitter
weeping, scarcely can one find a home untouched by the cruel hand of war.

'Abdu'l-Bahá, *Paris Talks*, pp. 114–15

Unity is of various kinds. Limited unities, such as unity based on a common language, a common nationality or a common race are no longer adequate in the present age. 'Abdu'l-Bahá defined two levels of unity that yield benefit to humankind today. The first is an intellectual realization that humanity is one interdependent organic whole; and so any harm that befalls one part of it affects all:

> The unity which is productive of unlimited results is first a unity of mankind which recognizes that all are sheltered beneath the overshadowing glory of the All-Glorious; that all are servants of one God; for all breathe the same atmosphere, live upon the same earth, move beneath the same heavens, receive effulgence from the same sun and are under the protection of one God. This is the most great unity, and its results are lasting if humanity adheres to it; but mankind has hitherto violated it, adhering to sectarian or other limited unities such as racial, patriotic or unity of self-interests; therefore no great results have been forthcoming. Nevertheless it is certain that the radiance and favours of God are encompassing, minds have developed, perceptions have become acute, sciences and arts are widespread and capacity exists for the proclamation and promulgation of the real and ultimate unity of mankind which will bring forth marvellous results.[6]

As our thinking becomes more universal, there gradually evolves within the individual a global consciousness, an awareness of the oneness of all humanity at the spiritual level. This results in a spiritual regeneration of humankind and in a higher level of unity, a spiritual unity, which is even more beneficial for humanity:

> Another unity is the spiritual unity which emanates from the breaths of the Holy Spirit. This is greater than the unity of mankind. Human unity or solidarity may be likened to the body whereas unity from the breaths of the Holy Spirit is the spirit animating the body. This is a perfect unity. It creates such a condition in mankind that each one will make sacrifices for the other and the utmost desire will be to forfeit life and all that pertains to it in behalf of another's good . . . This unity is the very spirit of the body of the world . . . His Holiness Jesus Christ . . . promulgated this unity among mankind. Every soul who believed in Jesus Christ became revivified and resuscitated through this spirit, attained to the zenith of eternal glory, realized the life everlasting, experienced the second birth and rose to the acme of good fortune.[7]

We should not think that this ideal of unity is one that is for others to pursue or something that is the responsibility of governments to bring about. Bahá'u'lláh makes it the duty of all of us as individuals to work for peace and unity:

> That one indeed is a man who, today, dedicateth himself to the service of the entire human race. The Great Being saith: Blessed and happy is he that ariseth to promote the best interests of the peoples and kindreds of the earth . . . The earth is but one country, and mankind its citizens.[8]

UNITY IN DIVERSITY

Consider the flowers of a garden. Though differing in kind, colour, form and shape, yet, inasmuch as they are refreshed by the waters of one spring, revived by the breath of one wind, invigorated by the rays of one sun, this diversity increaseth their charm and addeth unto their beauty. How unpleasing to the eye if all the flowers and plants, the leaves and blossoms, the fruit, the branches and the trees of that garden were all of the same shape and colour! Diversity of hues, form and shape enricheth and adorneth the garden, and heighteneth the effect thereof. In like manner, when divers shades of thought, temperament and character, are brought together under the power and influence of one central agency, the beauty and glory of human perfection will be revealed and made manifest. Naught but the celestial potency of the Word of God, which ruleth and transcendeth the realities of all things, is capable of harmonizing the divergent thoughts, sentiments, ideas and convictions of the children of men.

'Abdu'l-Bahá quoted in Shoghi Effendi,
World Order of Bahá'u'lláh, p. 42

Bahá'u'lláh calls upon his followers to put aside everything that causes dissension and division (such as religious, racial and national differences) and to come together in unity, to replace narrow parochial and partisan loyalties with a wider loyalty to the human race as a whole:

> Whatsoever hath led the children of men to shun one another, and hath caused dissensions and divisions amongst them, hath, through the revelation of these words, been nullified and abolished . . . Of old it hath been revealed: 'Love of one's country is an element of the Faith of God.' The Tongue of Grandeur hath, however, in the day of His manifestation proclaimed: 'It is not his to boast who loveth his country, but it is his who loveth the world.'[9]

Commenting on this last statement of Bahá'u'lláh, Shoghi Effendi declares that the Bahá'í teachings do not condemn a 'sane and intelligent patriotism in men's hearts'.[10] Indeed, he asserts that some degree of national autonomy is necessary in order to counter the evils of excessive centralization. There must, however, also be a wider loyalty, an aspiration to a higher universal level of unity.

Some people think that unity inevitably means uniformity. The Bahá'í aim, however, is to preserve the rich diversity of human language, culture, tradition and thought on this planet, while at the same time removing the causes of conflict and contention that exist. The mere fact that there are differences between people should not inevitably lead to dissension and strife. Looked at from another perspective, the existence of differences could be celebrated as a source of richness and variety. Shoghi Effendi states that the watchword of the Bahá'ís is 'unity in diversity'.[11]

Shoghi Effendi calls Bahá'u'lláh's teaching of the oneness of humankind the 'pivot round which all the teachings of Bahá'u'lláh revolve'.[12] He goes on to characterize it as being

> no mere outburst of ignorant emotionalism or an expression of vague and pious hope. Its appeal is not to be merely identified with a reawakening of the spirit of brotherhood and good-will among men, nor does it aim solely at the fostering of harmonious cooperation among individual peoples and nations . . . Its message is applicable not only to the individual, but concerns itself primarily with the nature of those essential relationships that must bind all the states and nations as members of one human family . . . It implies an organic change in the structure of present-day society, a change such as the world has not yet experienced . . . It calls for no less than the reconstruction and the demilitarization of the whole civilized world – a world organically unified in all the essential aspects of its life, its political machinery, its spiritual aspiration, its trade and finance, its script and language, and yet infinite in the diversity of the national characteristics of its federated units.[13]

WORLD ORDER

The coming together of the peoples of the world was impossible in previous ages. It is only with the development of modern means of communication that this is now possible.

In cycles gone by, though harmony was established, yet, owing to the absence of means, the unity of all mankind could not have been achieved. Continents remained widely divided, nay even among the peoples of one and the same continent association and interchange of thought were well nigh impossible. Consequently intercourse, understanding and unity amongst all the peoples and kindreds of the earth were unattainable. In this day, however, means of communication have multiplied, and the five continents of the earth have virtually merged into one. And for everyone it is now easy to travel to any land, to associate and exchange views with its peoples, and to become familiar, through publications, with the conditions, the religious beliefs and the thoughts of all men. ('Abdu'l-Bahá)[14]

'Abdu'l-Bahá states that these advances in human interaction have resulted in a situation of global interdependence:

In like manner all the members of the human family, whether peoples or governments, cities or villages, have become increasingly interdependent. For none is self-sufficiency any longer possible, inasmuch as political ties unite all peoples and nations, and the bonds of trade and industry, of agriculture and education, are being strengthened every day. Hence the unity of all mankind can in this day be achieved.[15]

The first stage in the achievement of world unity would be for the leaders of the world to come together and agree on peace. Bahá'u'lláh put forward the conditions for such a conference over a century ago:

The time must come when the imperative necessity for the holding of a vast, an all-embracing assemblage of men will be universally realized. The rulers and kings of the earth must needs attend it, and, participating in its deliberations, must consider such ways and means as will lay the foundations of the world's Great Peace amongst men.[16]

Such a conference must lead to a full conciliation of all disputes and provisions for mutually guaranteed security:

Such a peace demandeth that the Great Powers should resolve, for the sake of the tranquillity of the peoples of the earth, to be fully reconciled among themselves. Should any king take up arms against another, all should unitedly arise and prevent him. If this be done, the nations of the world will no longer require any armaments, except for the purpose of preserving the security of their realms and of maintaining internal order within their territories. This will ensure the peace and composure of every people, government and nation.[17]

Shoghi Effendi asserts that the result of such a process will be the establishment of a world commonwealth:

> The unity of the human race, as envisaged by Bahá'u'lláh, implies the establishment of a world commonwealth in which all nations, races, creeds and classes are closely and permanently united, and in which the autonomy of its state members and the personal freedom and initiative of the individuals that compose them are definitely and completely safeguarded.[18]

Eventually, however, it will be necessary for a number of international institutions to come into being. These will regulate international affairs so that wars will no longer be necessary. Shoghi Effendi outlines his vision of what will be needed as part of the world order:

> This commonwealth must, as far as we can visualize it, consist of:
>
> - A world legislature, whose members will, as the trustees of the whole of mankind, ultimately control the entire resources of all the component nations, and will enact such laws as shall be required to regulate the life, satisfy the needs and adjust the relationships of all races and peoples.
> - A world executive, backed by an international Force, will carry out the decisions arrived at, and apply the laws enacted by, this world legislature, and will safeguard the organic unity of the whole commonwealth.
> - A world tribunal will adjudicate and deliver its compulsory and final verdict in all and any disputes that may arise between the various elements constituting this universal system.
> - A mechanism of world inter-communication will be devised, embracing the whole planet, freed from national hindrances and restrictions, and functioning with marvellous swiftness and perfect regularity.
> - A world metropolis will act as the nerve centre of a world civilization, the focus towards which the unifying forces of life will converge and from which its energizing influences will radiate.
> - A world language will either be invented or chosen from among the existing languages and will be taught in the schools of all the federated nations as an auxiliary to their mother tongue.
> - A world script, a world literature, a uniform and universal system of currency, of weights and measures, will simplify and facilitate intercourse and understanding among the nations and races of mankind.[19]

Other features of this world commonwealth envisioned by Shoghi Effendi include:

> In such a world society, science and religion, the two most potent forces in human life, will be reconciled, will cooperate, and will harmoniously develop. The press will, under such a system, while giving full scope to the expression of the diversified views and convictions of mankind, cease to be mischievously manipulated by vested interests, whether private or public, and will be liberated from the influence of contending governments and peoples. The economic resources of the world will be organized, its sources of raw materials will be tapped and fully utilized, its markets will be coordinated and developed, and the distribution of its products will be equitably regulated.[20]

As the result of such a development, the Bahá'í writings envisage that the whole picture of the planet will be changed:

> National rivalries, hatred, and intrigues will cease, and racial animosity and prejudice will be replaced by racial amity, understanding and cooperation. The causes of religious strife will be permanently removed, economic barriers and restrictions will be completely abolished, and the inordinate distinction between classes will be obliterated. Destitution on the one hand, and gross accumulation of ownership on the other, will disappear. The enormous energy dissipated and wasted on war, whether economic or political, will be consecrated to such ends as will extend the range of human inventions and technical development, to the increase of the productivity of mankind, to the extermination of disease, to the extension of scientific research, to the raising of the standard of physical health, to the sharpening and refinement of the human brain, to the exploitation of the unused and unsuspected resources of the planet, to the prolongation of human life, and to the furtherance of any other agency that can stimulate the intellectual, the moral, and spiritual life of the entire human race. (Shoghi Effendi)[21]

To many people, passages such as the above may seem to depict an impossible utopia, and such people may regard Bahá'ís as dreamers and fools for imagining such an eventuality. A Bahá'í might reply that it is the Bahá'ís who are awake to the reality of our present global interdependence and the environmental, economic and social crises facing the world; that the vision of the future that they are advocating is the only one that will enable humanity to survive; and that the dreamers are those who imagine that humanity can survive if it continues on its present path, using inadequate political structures that were created in the nineteenth century (and did not even serve that century well) and adhering to such outworn political dogmas as unfettered national sovereignty.

SOCIAL AND ECONOMIC DEVELOPMENT

As indicated by its many social teachings, the religion of Bahá'u'lláh is not just concerned with the spiritual development of the individual. Its broad sweep includes a wide range of social principles and teachings that aim to carry forward humanity's collective life on this planet. An important aspect of this collective life is the need to develop every society and every group in society spiritually, socially and materially.

The field of social and economic development is usually associated with the poorer countries of the world. In the view of the Bahá'í teachings, however, there is no society that is not in urgent need of some aspect of the Bahá'í programme of development. Even the most affluent societies are suffering from grave problems, such as racism, substance abuse, crime, and a widening gulf between the advantaged and disadvantaged members of society. It is, nevertheless, the world's poorer nations that are the special focus of the development effort.

Many may think of the social and economic development of the poorer nations as rather remote from their day-to-day concerns. The Bahá'í teachings of the oneness of humankind imply, however, the development of a global consciousness that would require each person to think of every other person in the world as their brother or sister, or at least as their neighbour. This is a reflection of what is both physical reality (global mutual interdependence and interaction) and spiritual reality (the brotherhood and sisterhood of all human beings). The problems of those in the poorer nations of the world should therefore be the concern of those in the richer nations. Bahá'u'lláh, moreover, encourages his followers to concern themselves with just such problems: 'Be anxiously concerned with the needs of the age ye live in, and centre your deliberations on its exigencies and requirements.'[22] The concept that we are all trustees of the welfare of every other person on the planet is a theme that recurs frequently in the writings of Bahá'u'lláh and 'Abdu'l-Bahá.

The Bahá'í approach to social and economic development arises from two main considerations. The first, which has already been referred to above (p. 55), is the understanding that humankind is one organically whole entity. Thus whatever affects a part affects the whole. If one part of this entity is diseased, weak, or in distress, then the whole will suffer. The second consideration is that no plan for human development will ever succeed if it devotes itself solely to the physical aspects and neglects the spiritual. Many development projects are conceived with just economic and materialistic goals in view. The Bahá'í viewpoint is that for prosperity to be sustainable and equitable, attention must also be paid to the spiritual dimensions of the process. Only such considerations will lead to a progress that benefits all and is not damaging to the moral, social and environmental foundations of the community.

The immediate objectives of Bahá'í development projects may be tangible benefits (such as improved crops or the building of a school). There is, however, just as much concern that the project should be the outcome of universal consultation and participation and should result in a greater degree of unity in the community. Improvements in education, agriculture, literacy, and the status of women are all important goals. Equally important, however, are the moral and spiritual progress of the individuals in the community, the uprightness and probity of those entrusted with responsibilities, and the increased self-confidence and self-reliance of those who have been oppressed and downtrodden in society. The development of qualities such as trustworthiness, self-sacrifice and moral courage is just as important a goal as more tangible benefits.

An important principle in the Bahá'í attitude towards development planning is the need for the involvement of those for whom the plans are being made in the planning and execution of the task. For too long the rich have presumed to know what the poor need and have set about providing this, without consulting the intended recipients of their aid. The Bahá'í Faith proceeds on the basis of the equality of all human beings and the process of consultation (see pp. 78–80) among all involved. Communities are, therefore, encouraged to identify their own needs and initiate their own projects, which are then supported as needed by national and international Bahá'í bodies.

The unity of humankind, envisaged in the Bahá'í scriptures (see pp. 54–9), can only come about if there is also justice in the world. As long as people feel unfairly treated, there will be dissatisfaction and dissension in society:

The light of men is Justice. Quench it not with the contrary winds of oppression and tyranny. The purpose of justice is the appearance of unity among men . . . Were mankind to be adorned with this raiment, they would behold the day-star of the utterance, 'On that day God will satisfy everyone out of His abundance,' shining resplendent above the horizon of the world . . . Verily I say, whatever is sent down from the heaven of the Will of God is the means for the establishment of order in the world and the instrument for promoting unity and fellowship among its peoples. (Bahá'u'lláh)[23]

For too long have the rich and powerful individuals in society and the rich and powerful countries in the world manipulated international structures and development projects to their own advantage. This has led to a great deal of justifiable cynicism on the part of the poor towards the rich. The Bahá'í Faith teaches that only if there is consultation and collective decision making in which all participate and which is guided by the dictates of justice, can the requisite degree of unity of purpose and action be achieved to ensure a successful conclusion. Bahá'u'lláh links the principle of unity with the ideal of justice and the tool of consultation (see pp. 78–80) in a statement that summarizes the way in which personal morality and social action are linked: 'Say: no man can attain his true station except through his justice. No power can exist except through unity. No welfare and no well-being can be attained except through consultation.'[24]

One of the social principles that is advocated in the Bahá'í writings and is closely associated with the principle of social justice is the abolition of extremes of poverty and wealth. This is to be achieved not by any communist programme of forcible redistribution of wealth, but by directing resources at the problem. We have the means available to solve most of these problems thanks to the progress of science and technology. At present, this is used to produce goods for a small proportion of the people of the world and to generate profits for a tiny elite. The challenge for humanity is to harness this potential and to channel it towards those who really need it. A reordering of priorities and a reformation of the economic structures of the world are needed. But underlying this is the necessity for a new morality built on a different, more spiritual assessment of what human beings are.

One example of the sort of measures that characterize the Bahá'í effort towards this goal of social and economic development is the voluntary wealth tax called Ḥuqúqu'lláh. Each Bahá'í who manages to accumulate a certain amount of wealth (i.e. income that is in excess of necessary expenditure) voluntarily contributes 19 per cent of this to the World Centre of the Bahá'í Faith. This money is then used in whatever way the World Centre determines. In practice much of the money is in effect transferred from the richer countries to the Bahá'í communities in the poorer countries of the world. This transfer is thus achieved without any strings attached by the donor. Its use is decided using consultative processes usually involving the Bahá'í administrations in those countries, thus making it less likely that the money will be misused.

Apart from the payment of Ḥuqúqu'lláh, all Bahá'ís are also involved to some degree in social and economic development insofar as they participate in building up the Bahá'í administrative order. This is in itself a tool for development in that it enables local communities to consult widely and organize themselves to be able to carry out plans (see, for example, the list of the responsibilities of Local and National Spiritual Assemblies, pp. 69–70).

5 THE BAHÁ'Í COMMUNITY

The Bahá'í teachings contain many high principles and ideals. The Bahá'í community represents the attempt to put these principles into action. The principles of Bahá'í community life were laid down by Bahá'u'lláh and 'Abdu'l-Bahá, but it was in the time of Shoghi Effendi that most of its structure was actualized. This structure consists of a number of institutions which administer the Bahá'í community.

These Bahá'í institutions are necessary because the Bahá'í Faith has no clergy and no professional learned class. Bahá'u'lláh asserted that priests and other religious professionals had their role in former times when the majority of people were illiterate and needed guidance. Today, however, humanity has the ability to bring education and literacy to all. Therefore it is possible for all to read the scriptures themselves and come to their own understanding of them. Bahá'u'lláh has therefore abolished the priesthood and the professional religious class. It is still necessary, however, to fill the other function of religious professionals: the organization and administration of the community. The Bahá'í administrative order fulfils this function.

STRUCTURES

Nineteen Day Feast

The basis for the functioning of each local Bahá'í community is the Nineteen Day Feast. This event is held every nineteen days on the first day of each Bahá'í month (see Bahá'í calendar, p. 73 below). All the

Bahá'ís of an area must try to attend it. The meeting itself is divided into three parts. The first is a devotional portion at which prayers and passages from the holy writings are read. After this, there is an administrative part of the meeting during which there is usually a short report about the affairs of the Bahá'í Faith in the area. A very important aspect of this part of the meeting is a general consultation among the gathered Bahá'ís about issues that may be raised by any individual. The third part of this meeting is a social portion at which refreshments are served. At present, in many smaller Bahá'í communities, the Nineteen Day Feast is held in the home of one of the Bahá'ís and the host is responsible for the refreshments. This basic pattern of the Nineteen Day Feast can be adapted around the world to accommodate cultural differences.

The Local and National Spiritual Assemblies

The Bahá'ís in each area gather once a year during the Bahá'í holy day of Ridván (21 April, see p. 74) to hold an election. They elect nine of their number to be the Local Spiritual Assembly for the area. This assembly is the co-ordinating body of the Bahá'ís in that area. In a small Bahá'í community, it is usually just responsible for organizing activities to spread the Bahá'í Faith; arranging holy day celebrations and Nineteen Day Feasts; administering a local Bahá'í fund; and acting as an intermediary between the National Spiritual Assembly (see below) and the individual Bahá'ís. In larger Bahá'í communities, its role is more extensive (see below).

The next level up in the Bahá'í administrative hierarchy is the National Spiritual Assembly. This is formed in any country where there are sufficient Local Spiritual Assemblies. Delegates are elected to a National Convention, at which the National Spiritual Assembly is elected. In some parts of the world, however, there is not a sufficiently strong foundation of Local Spiritual Assemblies. Here, several countries may be grouped together under one Assembly, which is then often called a Regional Spiritual Assembly. Alternatively, some countries are divided into more than one 'National' Spiritual Assembly (the United States of America, for example, has one assembly for the continental USA, and one each for Hawaii and Alaska). Some colonies and dependent territories also have their own 'National' Spiritual Assemblies.

Within its area of jurisdiction, each National Spiritual Assembly is responsible for stimulating and co-ordinating the activities of Local

Spiritual Assemblies and individual Bahá'ís. It is also the main channel of communication between the Bahá'ís in its area and the Bahá'í World Centre.

◆

DUTIES OF THE MEMBERS OF SPIRITUAL ASSEMBLIES

Concerning the duties laid upon the members of Local and National Spiritual Assemblies, Shoghi Effendi writes:

Let it be made clear to every inquiring reader that among the most outstanding and sacred duties incumbent upon those who have been called upon to initiate, direct and coordinate the affairs of the Cause, are those that require them to win by every means in their power the confidence and affection of those whom it is their privilege to serve.

• Theirs is the duty to investigate and acquaint themselves with the considered views, the prevailing sentiments, the personal convictions of those whose welfare it is their solemn obligation to promote.
• Theirs is the duty to purge once for all their deliberations and the general conduct of their affairs from that air of self-contained aloofness, from the suspicion of secrecy, the stifling atmosphere of dictatorial assertiveness, in short, from every word and deed that might savour of partiality, self-centredness and prejudice.
• Theirs is the duty, while retaining the sacred and exclusive right of final decision in their hands, to invite discussion, provide information, ventilate grievances, welcome advice from even the most humble and insignificant members of the Bahá'í Family, expose their motives, set forth their plans, justify their actions,revise if necessary their verdict, foster the spirit of individual initiative and enterprise, and fortify the sense of interdependence and co-partnership, of understanding and mutual confidence between them on one hand and all local Assemblies and individual believers on the other.

Compilation of Compilations, vol. 2, no. 1463, pp. 108–9

◆

Within its area of jurisdiction, each Spiritual Assembly, whether local or national, is responsible for a wide range of functions such as:

• the promotion of the Bahá'í Faith
• the expansion and consolidation of the Bahá'í community
• the defence of the Bahá'í Faith against attacks made upon it
• the collection and disbursement of a Bahá'í fund
• the publication and distribution of Bahá'í literature
• the organization of child education and youth activities

- the administration of social and economic development projects by the Bahá'í community (for example, projects promoting education, the advancement of women or racial unity)
- the provision of humanitarian assistance to the sick and needy
- the representation of the Bahá'ís of an area in all their activities and relationships with Bahá'ís in other communities, and with the appropriate governmental and non-governmental organizations, agencies, and associations
- the promotion of the study of the Bahá'í writings and the strengthening and better functioning of the Bahá'í institutions
- the supervision of Bahá'í marriages, divorces, and funerals
- the arbitration and settlement of differences among members of the community

The Assembly can carry out these functions directly or through committees or individuals appointed by the Assembly.

The Universal House of Justice

The Universal House of Justice is elected by all of the members of all National Spiritual Assemblies at an International Convention. At present, this is held every five years. The Universal House of Justice is the supreme authority in the Bahá'í world and is, according to 'Abdu'l-Bahá, 'the source of all good and freed from all error'.[1] It is the supreme legislative authority of the Bahá'í Faith and is empowered to legislate on any areas that are not explicitly covered in the Bahá'í scriptures.

> The men of God's House of Justice have been charged with the affairs of the people. They, in truth, are the Trustees of God among His servants and the dayprings of authority in His countries . . . Inasmuch as for each day there is a new problem and for every problem an expedient solution, such affairs should be referred to the Ministers of the House of Justice that they may act according to the needs and requirements of the time . . . It is incumbent upon all to be obedient unto them. (Bahá'u'lláh)[2]

Many of the responsibilities and duties of the Universal House of Justice mirror on a global scale the general duties of the Local and National Spiritual Assemblies which are outlined in the previous section. Other specific responsibilities include:

- promoting peace and amity among the nations
- ensuring that no body or institution within the Bahá'í community abuses its privileges
- safeguarding the rights, freedom and initiative of the individual
- developing the Bahá'í World Centre and the administrative institutions of the Bahá'í Faith
- adjudicating in disputes referred to it by Local or National Spiritual Assemblies or by individuals
- preserving and safeguarding the sacred texts of the Bahá'í Faith[3]

Although the Universal House of Justice is the supreme authority in the Bahá'í world and its directives are therefore binding upon all Bahá'ís, any decisions made by the Universal House of Justice can subsequently, when circumstances change, be abrogated or changed by a further decision of the Universal House of Justice. (On women and the Universal House of Justice, see chapter 3.)

The appointed institutions of the Bahá'í Faith

As well as the above elected institutions, there are some institutions to which individual Bahá'ís may be appointed. Shoghi Effendi appointed a number of individuals to the position of Hand of the Cause. He gave these persons the task of promoting the expansion of the Bahá'í Faith and defending it against attacks. Since the death of Shoghi Effendi, no further Hands of the Cause can be appointed. Their functions, however, have been perpetuated through the creation of a number of institutions to which individual Bahá'ís are appointed for limited terms. The central institution of this appointed arm of the Bahá'í administration is the International Teaching Centre, which is based in Haifa. This institution supervises Continental Boards of Counsellors based in the different continents. These in turn appoint members of the Auxiliary Boards, which are responsible for a country or a part of a country. These Auxiliary Board members can, in turn, appoint assistants to help them in their tasks.

This appointed arm of the Bahá'í administration has no administrative powers or authority. It functions to stimulate and encourage the individual Bahá'ís and in a consultative capacity with the elected institutions.

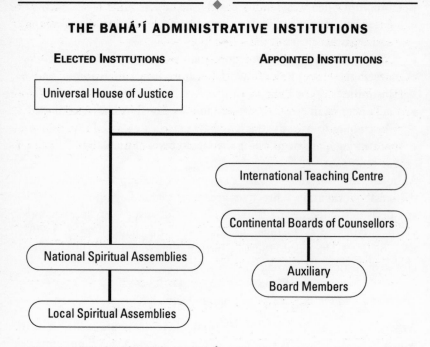

THE BAHÁ'Í ADMINISTRATIVE INSTITUTIONS

ELECTED INSTITUTIONS **APPOINTED INSTITUTIONS**

- Universal House of Justice
- International Teaching Centre
- Continental Boards of Counsellors
- National Spiritual Assemblies
- Auxiliary Board Members
- Local Spiritual Assemblies

The Bahá'í World Centre

The World Centre of the Bahá'í Faith is in the Haifa–Akka area. Here are situated the holiest shrines of the Bahá'í world: the shrine of Bahá'u'lláh at Bahjí just outside Akka and the shrine of the Báb (which at present also contains the shrine of 'Abdu'l-Bahá) situated on the side of Mount Carmel in the city of Haifa.

Adjacent to the shrine of the Báb in Haifa is a semicircular pathway, known as 'the arc', on which are the main administrative buildings of the World Centre. When completed these will include:

- the seat of the Universal House of Justice
- the seat of the International Teaching Centre
- the International Bahá'í Archives
- the Centre for the Study of the Sacred Texts
- the International Bahá'í Library

The Bahá'í World Centre also consists of several buildings, which were the residences of Bahá'u'lláh and 'Abdu'l-Bahá during their lives, and extensive gardens around these buildings.

Most of the holy places of the Bahá'í world are at the Bahá'í World Centre in the Haifa–Akka area and in Iran, Iraq and Turkey. These are places linked to the lives of the central figures of the religion. Those Bahá'ís who can afford to do so without difficulty are encouraged to perform a pilgrimage to them. The holy places in Iran and Iraq, however, cannot at present be visited due to persecution of the Bahá'í Faith in those countries.

The Bahá'í calendar

All the calendars now in widespread use in the world are closely associated with one or other of the world religions. Bahá'u'lláh introduced a new calendar, beginning from AD 1844.

MONTHS OF THE BAHÁ'Í YEAR

Bahá'í month	Translation	Begins
Bahá	Splendour	21 March
Jalál	Glory	9 April
Jamál	Beauty	28 April
'Azamat	Grandeur	17 May
Núr	Light	5 June
Rahmat	Mercy	24 June
Kalimát	Words	13 July
Kamál	Perfection	1 August
Asmá'	Names	20 August
'Izzat	Might	8 September
Mashíyyat	Will	27 September
'Ilm	Knowledge	16 October
Qudrat	Power	4 November
Qawl	Speech	23 November
Masá'il	Questions	12 December
Sharaf	Honour	31 December
Sultán	Sovereignty	19 January
Mulk	Dominion	7 February
'Alá'	Loftiness	2 March

The Bahá'í calendar was called by Bahá'u'lláh the Badí' (wondrous) calendar. Each year consists of nineteen months of nineteen days each. The year begins with the spring equinox on 21 March. The Bahá'í months are named after various spiritual qualities or divine attributes.

There are four additional (intercalary) days before the last month of the year ('Alá') which make the number of days up to 365. They are increased to five days in a leap year. These days are called the Ayyám-i-Há and are specially set aside for hospitality and the giving of presents.

Bahá'ís have nine holy days, most of which commemorate significant events in Bahá'í history. (For historical information on these events, see chapter 8.) Wherever possible, Bahá'ís suspend work on these days.

◆

BAHÁ'Í HOLY DAYS

Naw-Rúz (New Year)	21 March
Ridván – first day	21 April
Ridván – ninth day	29 April
Ridván – twelfth day	2 May
The Báb's declaration of his mission	23 May
Passing of Bahá'u'lláh	29 May
Martyrdom of the Báb	9 July
Birth of the Báb	20 October
Birth of Bahá'u'lláh	12 November

◆

The House of Worship (Mashriqu'l-Adhkár)

At present, Bahá'ís in most local communities have no special place of worship. They meet either in each other's homes or at a Bahá'í centre. It is envisaged, however, that in the future there will be a House of Worship (Mashriqu'l-Adhkár) in each town. Around it will be built schools, universities, libraries, medical facilities, orphanages and so on. This will become the spiritual and social centre of the community.

The Bahá'í House of Worship is open to people of all backgrounds, not just Bahá'ís, in accordance with the Bahá'í aim of fostering unity. In his speech at the laying of the cornerstone of the Ma<u>sh</u>riqu'l-A<u>dh</u>kár in Wilmette, 'Abdu'l-Bahá stated that

> the original purpose of temples and houses of worship is simply that of unity--places of meeting where various peoples, different races and souls of every capacity may come together in order that love and agreement should be manifest between them . . . that all religions, races and sects may come together within its universal shelter.[4]

At present Bahá'ís prefer to use their money on other projects and, therefore, there are only seven of these Houses of Worship around the world as a symbol of future intentions. These seven are: near Chicago, USA; near Kampala, Uganda; near Sydney, Australia; near Frankfurt, Germany; near Panama City, Panama; near Apia, Samoa; and in New Delhi, India (see cover illustration).

PRINCIPLES OF BAHÁ'Í ADMINISTRATION

It is important to note that Bahá'ís do not regard the Bahá'í administration as merely a convenient way of organizing themselves. First, its key institutions and guiding principles have been established in the writings of the founders of the religion. Bahá'ís, therefore, consider the Bahá'í administration as sacred in nature and as integral a part of the Bahá'í Faith as the Bahá'í teachings; indeed the Bahá'í administration is seen as the incarnation of the spirit of the Bahá'í Faith. Second, Bahá'ís consider that the Bahá'í teachings can only flower fully within the institutional framework provided by the Bahá'í administration. The Bahá'í principles and teachings by themselves would remain ideas without the Bahá'í administration to give them form. Third, this administrative framework will, Bahá'ís believe, evolve gradually into a world order. When that occurs, it will be the fulfilment of the prophecies of every religion that there will be a golden age of peace and prosperity for humanity.

The structure of the Bahá'í administrative institutions, as described above, is unlike those of other religions. There are some principles governing their functioning also make them unlike other comparable institutions.

MERE PLANS ARE NOT SUFFICIENT

The Bahá'í administration is, Bahá'ís believe, the agency through which the Bahá'í teachings can be put into effect in the world. 'Abdu'l-Bahá spoke of the fact that mere good intentions and ideas are not enough; there is also the need for some way to put these into effect in the world:

Mere knowledge is not sufficient for complete human attainment... A house is not built by mere acquaintance with the plans. Money must be forthcoming; volition is necessary to construct it; a carpenter must be employed in its erection. It is not enough to say, "The plan and purpose of this house are very good; I will live in it.' There are no walls of protection, there is no roof of shelter in this mere statement; the house must be actually built before we can live in it...

Bahá'u'lláh not only proclaimed this unity and love; He established it. As a heavenly Physician He not only gave prescriptions for these ailments of discord and hatred but accomplished the actual healing. We may read in a medical book that a certain form of illness requires such and such a remedy. While this may be absolutely true, the remedy is useless unless there be volition and executive force to apply it...

It is, therefore, evident and proved that an effort must be put forward to complete the purpose and plan of the teachings of God in order that in this great Day of days the world may be reformed, souls resuscitated, a new spirit of life found, hearts become illumined, mankind rescued from the bondage of nature, saved from the baseness of materialism and attain spirituality and radiance in attraction toward the divine Kingdom. This is necessary; this is needful. Mere reading of the Holy Books and texts will not suffice.

Many years ago in Baghdad I saw a certain officer sitting upon the ground. Before him a large paper was placed into which he was sticking needles tipped with small red and white flags. First he would stick them into the paper, then thoughtfully pull them out and change their position. I watched him with curious interest for a long time, then asked, 'What are you doing?' He replied, "I have in mind something which is historically related of Napoleon I during his war against Austria. One day, it is said, his secretary found him sitting upon the ground as I am now doing, sticking needles into a paper before him. His secretary inquired what it meant. Napoleon answered, "I am on the battlefield figuring out my next victory. You see, Italy and Austria are defeated, and France is triumphant." In the great campaign which followed, everything came out just as he said. His army carried his plans to a complete success. Now, I am doing the same as Napoleon, figuring out a great campaign of military conquest.' I said, 'Where is your army? Napoleon had an army already equipped when he figured out his victory. You have no army. Your forces exist only on paper. You have no power to conquer countries. First get ready your army, then sit upon the ground with your needles.' We need an army to attain victory in the spiritual world; mere plans are not sufficient; ideas and principles are helpless without a divine power to put them into effect.

'Abdu'l-Bahá, *Promulgation of Universal Peace*, pp. 249–50

◆

The Covenant

The bedrock of the Bahá'í Faith is the principle of the Covenant. The Bahá'í Faith has very little in the way of dogmas or creed to which its adherents are required to subscribe. Each Bahá'í is guaranteed the freedom to interpret the Bahá'í scriptures according to his or her individual understanding: 'Let us also remember that at the very root of the Cause lies the principle of the undoubted right of the individual to self-expression, his freedom to declare his conscience and set forth his views' (Shoghi Effendi).[5] Such interpretative freedom would inevitably lead to doctrinal chaos and the formation of numerous sects based on the interpretations of various individuals if it were not for the existence of a Covenant or spiritual agreement into which each Bahá'í enters.

In brief this Covenant states that, while each individual is free to interpret the Bahá'í scriptures, no one may claim that theirs is the only correct interpretation or that it is in any way authoritative. Only the writings of Bahá'u'lláh and of the two authorized interpreters of the Bahá'í scriptures, 'Abdu'l-Bahá and Shoghi Effendi, are authoritative and binding.

Coupled with this agreement to refrain from claiming any authority for one's own views is an agreement to abide by the decisions and directives of the leader of the Bahá'í Faith, which, since its election in 1963, has been the Universal House of Justice. If any individual Bahá'í feels that any administrative decision made by either a Local Spiritual Assembly or a National Spiritual Assembly is wrong or unjust, he or she is free to appeal that decision all the way up to the Universal House of Justice. Once the Universal House of Justice has ruled on the issue,however, the matter is settled and there should be no further dissent. 'Abdu'l-Bahá has put this very emphatically. Referring to Shoghi Effendi and the Universal House of Justice, he states: 'Whatsoever they decide is of God. Whoso obeyeth him not, neither obeyeth them, hath not obeyed God; whoso rebelleth against him and against them hath rebelled against God . . . whoso contendeth with them hath contended with God.'[6]

The concept of the Covenant is the focal centre of the Bahá'í Faith and the source of its unity:

> The power of the Covenant will protect the Cause of Bahá'u'lláh from the doubts of the people of error. It is the fortified fortress of the Cause of God and the firm pillar of the religion of God. Today no power can conserve the oneness of the Bahá'í world save the Covenant of God; otherwise differences like unto a most great tempest will encompass the Bahá'í world. ('Abdu'l-Bahá)[7]

And since Bahá'ís believe that the teachings of Bahá'u'lláh are what will bring unity to the world, the Covenant, by maintaining the unity of the Bahá'í Faith, is 'the axis of the oneness of the world of humanity'.[8] Therefore, 'Abdu'l-Bahá says that:

> Today the pulsating power in the arteries of the body of the world is the spirit of the Covenant-the spirit which is the cause of life. Whosoever is vivified with this spirit, the freshness and beauty of life become manifest in him, he is baptized with the Holy Spirit, he is born again, is freed from oppression and tyranny, from heedlessness and harshness which deaden the spirit, and attains to everlasting life.[9]

Consultation

The mechanism by which decisions are made at all levels of the Bahá'í administrative order involves the process of consultation. The purpose of consultation is to bring the minds of several people to bear on a particular subject so that the decision made is the result of the group's collective wisdom.[10]

'Abdu'l-Bahá asserts that this result can only be achieved, however, if certain conditions are met:

> The prime requisites for them that take counsel together are purity of motive, radiance of spirit, detachment from all else save God, attraction to His Divine Fragrances, humility and lowliness amongst His loved ones, patience and long-suffering in difficulties and servitude to His exalted

Threshold. Should they be graciously aided to acquire these attributes, victory from the unseen Kingdom of Bahá shall be vouchsafed to them. . . he members [of a Spiritual Assembly] must take counsel together in such wise that no occasion for ill-feeling or discord may arise. This can be attained when every member expresseth with absolute freedom his own opinion and setteth forth his argument. Should any one oppose, he must on no account feel hurt for not until matters are fully discussed can the right way be revealed. The shining spark of truth cometh forth only after the clash of differing opinions. If after discussion, a decision be carried unanimously, well and good; but if the Lord forbid, differences of opinion should arise, a majority of voices must prevail.[11]

◆

'ABDU'L-BAHÁ ON CONSULTATION

In this Cause consultation is of vital importance, but spiritual conference and not the mere voicing of personal views is intended. In France I was present at a session of the senate, but the experience was not impressive. Parliamentary procedure should have for its object the attainment of the light of truth upon questions presented and not furnish a battleground for opposition and self-opinion. Antagonism and contradiction are unfortunate and always destructive to truth. In the parliamentary meeting mentioned, altercation and useless quibbling were frequent; the result, mostly confusion and turmoil; even in one instance a physical encounter took place between two members. It was not consultation but comedy.

The purpose is to emphasize the statement that consultation must have for its object the investigation of truth. He who expresses an opinion should not voice it as correct and right but set it forth as a contribution to the consensus of opinion, for the light of reality becomes apparent when two opinions coincide. A spark is produced when flint and steel come together. Man should weigh his opinions with the utmost serenity, calmness and composure. Before expressing his own views he should carefully consider the views already advanced by others. If he finds that a previously expressed opinion is more true and worthy, he should accept it immediately and not wilfully hold to an opinion of his own. By this excellent method he endeavours to arrive at unity and truth . . . Therefore, true consultation is spiritual conference in the attitude and atmosphere of love. Members must love each other in the spirit of fellowship in order that good results may be forthcoming. Love and fellowship are the foundation.

Promulgation of Universal Peace, pp. 72–3

◆

Nor is the tool of consultation only to be used in matters of Bahá'í administration. It is something that can be used whenever a decision has to be made:

> Consultation is acceptable in the presence of the Almighty, and hath been enjoined upon the believers, so that they may confer upon ordinary and personal matters, as well as on affairs which are general in nature and universal. For instance, when a man hath a project to accomplish, should he consult with some of his brethren, that which is agreeable will of course be investigated and unveiled to his eyes, and the truth will be disclosed. Likewise on a higher level, should the people of a village consult one another about their affairs, the right solution will certainly be revealed. In like manner, the members of each profession, such as in industry, should consult , and those in commerce should similarly consult on business affairs. In short, consultation is desirable and acceptable in all things and on all issues. ('Abdu'l-Bahá)[12]

Power and decentralization

It is a cardinal principle of the Bahá'í administration that power and authority does not reside in individuals but in elected institutions. Those individuals elected to be members of these institutions have no rank, power or authority as individuals. Although newspapers and other outside bodies may call individuals such as the chairperson of a National Spiritual Assembly 'the leader of the Bahá'í community' as a parallel with other religious groups, this is not a correct description. It is the institution that is the leader and not the individual. Although it is true that members of the appointed arm of the administration (see pp. 71–2 above) exercise their functions as individuals, these individuals have no administrative powers and act in an advisory capacity only.

Within the Bahá'í administration, it is also a principle to decentralize as much as it is feasible to do. Thus, for example, as soon as the National Spiritual Assemblies had developed sufficiently for them to take over the planning of the expansion and development of the Bahá'í Faith in their areas, this responsibility was given to them by the Universal House of Justice. Each Spiritual Assembly has jurisdiction and authority over all Bahá'í activity in its area of jurisdiction. It is subject to the authority of the next higher level in the hierarchy of elected institutions only when the activities it undertakes have an impact beyond the boundaries of its area of jurisdiction.

The Rights of Minorities

Importance is given in the Bahá'í administrative order to the protection of the rights of minorities: 'Every organized community enlisted under the banner of Bahá'u'lláh should feel it to be its first and inescapable obligation to nurture, encourage, and safeguard every minority belonging to any faith, race, class, or nation within it' (Shoghi Effendi).[13]

This can be seen as one aspect of the Bahá'í principles of the oneness of humanity and the need for the abolition of prejudices. The Bahá'í community goes further than merely acknowledging the equality of the members of minority groups, however-it encourages the positive participation of these minority groups in its affairs. Thus, for example, in the case of a tied vote in an election, priority should be accorded to the member of a minority group. Shoghi Effendi states:

> Bearing in mind the extreme desirability of having the minority elements participate and share responsibility in the conduct of Bahá'í activity, it should be the duty of every Bahá'í community so to arrange its affairs that in cases where individuals belonging to the divers minority elements within it are already qualified and fulfil the necessary requirements, Bahá'í representative institutions, be they Assemblies, conventions, conferences, or committees, may have represented on them as many of these divers elements, racial or otherwise, as possible. The adoption of such a course, and faithful adherence to it, would not only be a source of inspiration and encouragement to those elements that are numerically small and inadequately represented, but would demonstrate to the world at large the universality and representative character of the Faith of Bahá'u'lláh, and the freedom of His followers from the taint of those prejudices which have already wrought such havoc in the domestic affairs, as well as the foreign relationships, of the nations.[14]

Bahá'í elections

Elections to the Bahá'í administrative institutions take place by a free and secret ballot. They are, however, radically different from most other elections that take place in the world today. They are not the arena for a struggle for power between opposing individuals, policies, ideologies or parties. A prohibition on nominations, electioneering and the formation of parties helps to ensure this.

The process of election is considered to be a vehicle for choosing individuals who have the necessary moral, spiritual and administrative capabilities to consult together and co-operate to promote the common good. Those elected do not represent any particular interest or faction. They must see themselves as chosen for a service to the whole community, a service that they must perform prayerfully and conscientiously.

6 BAHÁ'Í LAWS

Nothing worthy of attainment can be achieved without discipline. We cannot hope to play a musical instrument well unless we submit ourselves to the discipline of hours of practice. The same is true in the spiritual realm. To progress spiritually, one must undergo a spiritual discipline. Bahá'u'lláh has introduced a number of laws for his followers to observe. Some of these, such as prayer, meditation and fasting, are to help the individual's spiritual progress; some, such as the marriage laws, have social implications.

One of the primary purposes of the laws, as well as the teachings, that Bahá'u'lláh has given is the uniting of the peoples of the world:

> O ye that dwell on earth! The distinguishing feature that marketh the preeminent character of this Supreme Revelation consisteth in that We have, on the one hand, blotted out from the pages of God's holy Book whatsoever hath been the cause of strife, of malice and mischief amongst the children of men, and have, on the other, laid down the essential prerequisites of concord, of understanding, of complete and enduring unity. Well is it with them that keep My statutes.[1]

In the West, people tend to see the law as something that limits their freedom and hence something that is only to be endured reluctantly because there is some indirect overall benefit. In the Bahá'í Faith, however, there is a more positive attitude towards the law instituted by Bahá'u'lláh. It enables human beings to align themselves with the spiritual laws that govern the universe. We would not jump from a fourth-storey window, because we know that the physical laws of the universe would cause us to injure ourselves badly. Similarly, Bahá'ís believe that we should not break these spiritual laws, otherwise we should inflict spiritual harm upon ourselves. Bahá'u'lláh, therefore, does not present these laws as a rigid legalistic framework, concerned with enforcement and punishment. He states that these laws are an indispensable part of a human being's spiritual progress; signposts on the mystic path: 'Think not that We have revealed unto you a mere code of laws. Nay, rather, We have unsealed the choice Wine with the fingers of might and power.'² And so obedience to these laws should not be for fear of punishment, but out of joy and love: 'Observe My commandments, for the love of My beauty.'³

PRAYER, READING OF SCRIPTURE AND MEDITATION

Part of the spiritual discipline that Bahá'u'lláh has given to his followers is to spend time every day in carrying out spiritual exercises. One of these is daily obligatory prayer. There are three obligatory prayers and a Bahá'í is free to choose any one of them to say daily. There are also many other prayers which one can use as part of one's devotions.

Bahá'u'lláh has also instructed his followers to read a passage of the scripture and meditate upon it twice a day, morning and evening. It is not the physical action of performing these spiritual disciplines that is important, but rather the spirit in which they are done. The intention should be to turn away from the world and towards the spiritual realm. It is the quality of the time spent in this way that is important, not the quantity:

> Pride not yourselves on much reading of the verses or on a multitude of pious acts by day and night. For were a man to read a single verse with joy and radiance it would be better for him than to read with lassitude all the Holy Books of God . . . Read ye the holy verses in such measure that ye be not overcome by languor and despondency. Lay not upon your souls that which will weary them and weigh them down, but rather what will lighten and uplift them. (Bahá'u'lláh)⁴

When asked why it is important for human beings to pray, 'Abdu'l-Bahá replied:

> O thou spiritual friend! Thou hast asked the wisdom of prayer. Know thou that prayer is indispensable and obligatory, and man under no

PRAYER

The short obligatory prayer – to be said once daily between noon and sunset

I bear witness, O my God, that Thou hast created me to know Thee and to worship Thee. I testify, at this moment, to my powerlessness and to Thy might, to my poverty and to Thy wealth.
     There is none other God but Thee the Help in Peril, the Self-Subsisting.

Prayers and Meditations, no. 181, p. 314

Other prayers

Is there any remover of difficulties save God? Say: Praised be God! He is God! All are His servants and all abide by His bidding.

The Báb, *Bahá'í Prayers*, p. 28

O my God! O my God! Unite the hearts of Thy servants, and reveal to them Thy great purpose. May they follow Thy commandments and abide in Thy law. Help them, O God in their endeavour, and grant them strength to serve Thee. O God! Leave them not to themselves, but guide their steps by the light of knowledge and cheer their hearts by Thy love. Verily, Thou art their Helper and their Lord.

Bahá'u'lláh, *Bahá'í Prayers*, p. 204

Create in me a pure heart, O my God, and renew a tranquil conscience within me, O my Hope! Through the spirit of power confirm Thou me in Thy Cause, O my Best-Beloved, and by the light of Thy glory reveal unto me Thy path, O Thou the Goal of my desire! Through the power of Thy transcendent might lift me up unto the heaven of Thy holiness, O Source of my being, and by the breezes of Thine eternity gladden me, O Thou Who art my God! Let Thine everlasting melodies breathe tranquillity on me, O my Companion, and let the riches of Thine ancient countenance deliver me from all except Thee, O my Master, and let the tidings of the revelation of Thine incorruptible Essence bring me joy, O Thou Who art the most manifest of the manifest and the most hidden of the hidden!

Bahá'u'lláh, *Bahá'í Prayers*, pp. 142–3

O God! Refresh and gladden my spirit. Purify my heart. Illumine my powers. I lay all my affairs in Thy hand. Thou art my Guide and Refuge. I will no longer be full of anxiety, nor will I let trouble harass me. I will not dwell on the unpleasant things of life.
     O God! Thou art more friend to me than I am to myself. I dedicate myself to Thee, O Lord.

'Abdu'l-Bahá, *Bahá'í Prayers*, p. 152

pretext whatsoever is excused from performing the prayer unless he be mentally unsound, or an insurmountable obstacle prevent him. The wisdom of prayer is this: That it causeth a connection between the servant and the True One, because in that state man with all heart and soul turneth his face towards His Highness the Almighty, seeking His association and desiring His love and compassion. The greatest happiness for a lover is to converse with his beloved, and the greatest gift for a seeker is to become familiar with the object of his longing; that is why with every soul who is attracted to the Kingdom of God, his greatest hope is to find an opportunity to entreat and supplicate before his Beloved, appeal for His mercy and grace and be immersed in the ocean of His utterance, goodness and generosity.

Besides all this, prayer and fasting is the cause of awakening and mindfulness and conducive to protection and preservation from tests.[5]

◆

MEDITATION

While you meditate you are speaking with your own spirit. In that state of mind you put certain questions to your spirit and the spirit answers: the light breaks forth and the reality is revealed.

You cannot apply the name 'man' to any being void of this faculty of meditation; without it he would be a mere animal, lower than the beasts.

Through the faculty of meditation man attains to eternal life; through it he receives the breath of the Holy Spirit – the bestowal of the Spirit is given in reflection and meditation. The spirit of man is itself informed and strengthened during meditation; through it affairs of which man knew nothing are unfolded before his view. Through it he receives Divine inspiration, through it he receives heavenly food.

Meditation is the key for opening the doors of mysteries. In that state man abstracts himself: in that state man withdraws himself from all outside objects; in that subjective mood he is immersed in the ocean of spiritual life and can unfold the secrets of things-in-themselves. To illustrate this, think of man as endowed with two kinds of sight; when the power of insight is being used the outward power of vision does not see. This faculty of meditation frees man from the animal nature, discerns the reality of things, puts man in touch with God.

This faculty brings forth from the invisible plane the sciences and arts. Through the meditative faculty inventions are made possible, colossal undertakings are carried out; through it governments can run smoothly. Through this faculty man enters into the very Kingdom of God.

Nevertheless some thoughts are useless to man; they are like waves moving in the sea without result. But if the faculty of meditation is bathed in the inner light and characterized with divine attributes, the results will be confirmed.

The meditative faculty is akin to the mirror; if you put it before earthly objects it will reflect them. Therefore if the spirit of man is contemplating earthly subjects he will be informed of these. But if you turn the mirror of your spirits heavenwards, the heavenly constellations and the rays of the Sun of Reality will be reflected in your hearts, and the virtues of the Kingdom will be obtained.

Therefore let us keep this faculty rightly directed-turning it to the heavenly Sun and not to earthly objects-so that we may discover the secrets of the Kingdom, and comprehend the allegories of the Bible and the mysteries of the spirit.

May we indeed become mirrors reflecting the heavenly realities, and may we become so pure as to reflect the stars of heaven.

'Abdu'l-Bahá, *Paris Talks*, pp. 174–6

◆

Although the Bahá'í writings urge one to meditate, there is no set form for meditation prescribed. One is therefore free to use whatever method one prefers. Some Bahá'ís confine themselves to reading a passage of scripture and meditating upon it. Some use a particular method of meditation.

As an adjunct to prayer and meditation, there are short short phrases given by Bahá'u'lláh and more particularly by the Báb. These can be chanted in the same way as mantras or the Sufi *dhikr*. Bahá'u'lláh, for example, instructs that the phrase 'Alláhu Abhá' (God is most glorious!) should be said ninety-five times each day.

Prayers can be said or chanted or even set to music:

Among some of the nations of the Orient, music and harmony was not approved of, but the Manifested Light, Bahá'u'lláh, in this glorious period has revealed in Holy Tablets that singing and music are the spiritual food of the hearts and souls. In this dispensation, music is one of the arts that is highly approved and is considered to be the cause of the exaltation of sad and desponding hearts.

Therefore . . . set to music the verses and the divine words so that they may be sung with soul-stirring melody in the Assemblies and gatherings, and that the hearts of the listeners may become tumultuous and rise towards the Kingdom of Abhá in supplication and prayer. ('Abdu'l-Bahá)[6]

FASTING

Apart from prayer and meditation, the other major spiritual discipline or tool for spiritual advancement is fasting. Bahá'ís fast from sunrise to sunset for nineteen days of the year (2 March to 20 March). This is a period of spiritual regeneration.

> It is essentially a period of meditation and prayer, of spiritual recuperation, during which the believer must strive to make the necessary readjustments in his inner life, and to refresh and reinvigorate the spiritual forces latent in his soul. Its significance and purpose are, therefore, fundamentally spiritual in character. (Shoghi Effendi)[7]

Indeed, fasting is a symbol of our desire to become detached from the things of this world:

> For this material fast is an outer token of the spiritual fast; it is a symbol of self-restraint, the withholding of oneself from all appetites of the self, taking on the characteristics of the spirit, being carried away by the breathings of heaven and catching fire from the love of God. ('Abdu'l-Bahá)[8]

MARRIAGE AND DIVORCE

Marriage is considered in the Bahá'í Faith to be one of the most important social institutions. 'And when He [God] desired to manifest grace and beneficence to men, and to set the world in order, He revealed observances and created laws: among them He established the law of marriage, made it as a fortress for well-being and salvation.'[9]

Marriage, although enjoined and highly recommended, is not obligatory. Bahá'í law allows only monogamous marriage between a man and a woman. The taking of more than one wife or husband at a time is prohibited. While many religions condemn all expressions of sexuality as being in some way base, the Bahá'í Faith 'recognizes the value of the sex impulse'[10] but asserts that sexuality may only legitimately be expressed within marriage, (see also pp. 25–7).

Marriage must be with the free consent of the couple. To make marriage a stronger source of social cohesion, Bahá'u'lláh has also made it conditional upon the consent of their parents. He states that this is in order 'to establish love, unity and harmony amidst Our servants'.[11]

The Bahá'í marriage ceremony has no set form to it. Each couple can therefore arrange their wedding ceremony according to their own wishes and can incorporate any features of their local culture that would be appropriate. The only set part of the ceremony is the exchange before witnesses of the marriage vow: 'We will all, verily, abide by the Will of God.'

It is customary in many parts of the world to give dowries and these frequently cause much conflict and distress, either because the giver is unable to afford it or the receiver considers the amount too small. Bahá'u'lláh addressed these problems by fixing the amount of dowries.

Divorce is strongly condemned. It is only permitted if there is irreconcilable differences and antipathy between the two parties. Several conditions must be met, including a year of separation during which efforts are made to effect a reconciliation.

A PRAYER FOR MARRIAGE

Glory be unto Thee, O my God! Verily, this Thy servant and this Thy maidservant have gathered under the shadow of Thy mercy and are united through Thy favour and generosity. O Lord! Confirm them in Thy servitude and assist them in Thy service. Suffer them to become the signs of Thy name in Thy world and protect them through Thy bestowals which are inexhaustible in this world and the world to come. O Lord! They are supplicating the kingdom of Thy mercifulness and invoking the realm of Thy singleness. Verily, they are married in obedience to Thy command. Cause them to become the signs of harmony and unity until the end of time. Verily, Thou art the Omnipotent and the Almighty!

'Abdu'l-Bahá, *Bahá'í Prayers*, pp. 45–6

DEATH AND BURIAL

Death is regarded by Bahá'ís as a stage in one's eternal life. It is the point that marks one's passage to the next world (see chapter 7). The body that has been the temple with which the human soul has been associated should be treated with respect and the funeral ceremonies carried out 'with dignity and honour'.[12] Cremation is forbidden. 'Abdu'l-Bahá explains that, according to the natural order of things, the body should be allowed to decompose gradually.[13] There is a specific prayer that should be said at funerals. There are also other prayers that may be said at the funeral or at a later time for the dead person's spiritual progress in the next world (see chapter 7).

Bahá'ís are instructed to each write a will and are free to dispose of their wealth in any way they wish. Bahá'u'lláh has prescribed a division of wealth for those who die without leaving a will.

CRUELTY TO ANIMALS

Bahá'u'lláh has enjoined kindness to animals[14] and has specifically condemned burdening an animal with more than it can bear.[15]

Because animals do not have the power of speech, 'Abdu'l-Bahá states that they are to be treated with even more consideration than are people:

> Ye do worse to harm an animal, for man hath a language, he can lodge a complaint, he can cry out and moan; if injured he can have recourse to the authorities and these will protect him from his aggressor. But the hapless beast is mute, able neither to express its hurt nor take its case to the authorities. If a man inflict a thousand ills upon a beast, it can neither ward him off with speech nor hale him into court. Therefore is it essential that ye show forth the utmost consideration to the animal, and that ye be even kinder to him than to your fellow man.[16]

ABOLITIONS AND PROHIBITIONS

A number of doctrines and practices which have grown up in various religions have been specifically abolished by Bahá'u'lláh. These include: the priesthood; the waging of holy war; asceticism and monasticism; the confession of sins; the burning of books; the use of pulpits; and regarding certain people or things as impure.

Bahá'u'lláh prohibited his followers from taking part in a number of activities including: slavery; begging; the kissing of hands; the taking of intoxicating drugs and alcohol; gambling; carrying arms unnecessarily; and homosexuality.

Some other laws, such as the Huqúqu'lláh, are referred to elsewhere (see pp. 65–6).

7 THEOLOGICAL TEACHINGS

The Bahá'í teachings for the individual and for society have been given in the previous chapters. It should never be forgotten, however, that the Bahá'í Faith is a religion and that underlying these ethical and social teachings is a spiritual and mystical teaching, which in turn is based on certain theological assumptions.

THE NATURE OF THE HIGHEST REALITY (GOD)

In the Western religions, the highest reality is called God. In these religions, God is the creator of all that is. He is the Lord of all, who intervenes in human affairs and sends His prophets to bring laws and teachings to humanity. The duty of human beings is to recognize the prophet and to lead their lives according to these laws and teachings.

In the religions of the East, the highest reality has different characteristics. Whether we consider Nirvana or the Dharma in Theravada Buddhism, Shunyata in Mahayana Buddhism, the Tao in Taoism, or Brahma in Advaita Hinduism, the highest reality in these Eastern religions does not have the personal characteristics of God in the Western religions; it is impersonal in the sense that it does not exercise a will, and does not intervene in human affairs. Rather, this highest reality is seen as the Absolute Reality of which our worldly reality is an aspect. If human beings could see things as they really are, they would recognize that their reality and the Absolute Reality are one and the same. This is expressed by various formulae in these religions, such as the truth that

Atman (the individual soul) is Brahman (Absolute Reality) in Advaita Hinduism, or that Samsara (the contingent world) is Nirvana (the Absolute) in Buddhism.

Bahá'u'lláh's teaching about the highest reality starts with the basic statement that an absolute knowledge of this reality is impossible for human beings to achieve. The finite nature of the human mind cannot grasp and comprehend the infinite:

> So perfect and comprehensive is His creation that no mind or heart, however keen or pure, can ever grasp the nature of the most insignificant of His creatures; much less fathom the mystery of Him Who is the Day Star of Truth, Who is the invisible and unknowable Essence.[1]

Since no absolute knowledge of the highest reality is available, all descriptions, all schemata, all attempts to portray the highest reality are necessarily limited by the point of view of the particular person making them. They are limited, relative truths only:

> All that the sages and mystics have said or written have never exceeded, nor can they ever hope to exceed, the limitations to which man's finite mind hath been strictly subjected. To whatever heights the mind of the most exalted of men may soar, however great the depths which the detached and understanding heart can penetrate, such mind and heart *can never transcend that which is the creature of their own thoughts*. The meditations of the profoundest thinker, the devotions of the holiest of saints, the highest expressions of praise from either human pen or tongue, are but *a reflection of that which hath been created within themselves.* (Bahá'u'lláh; emphasis added)[2]

Therefore, although the religions of the East and West have widely differing concepts of the highest reality, Bahá'u'lláh maintains that this does not mean that there is a difference in the reality that is being described. Rather, the religions differ because they are each looking at that reality from a different viewpoint. They have each constructed concepts and ideas from their own perspective. The source of the differences lies, therefore, not in what is being observed; rather, it lies in the fact that those who have written on these subjects have each had a particular cultural or personal background that predetermines the way that they have looked at these matters: 'The differences among the religions of the world are due to the varying types of minds' ('Abdu'l-Bahá).[3]

'Abdu'l-Bahá has summarized this teaching by saying that whatever it is that all peoples, whether of the East or the West, have conceptualized, it is a product of their own minds and therefore limited by their minds. It can therefore never encompass the infinite and unlimited nature of God or Absolute Reality:

> This people, all of them, have pictured a god in the realm of the mind, and worship that image which they have made for themselves. And yet that image is comprehended, the human mind being the comprehender thereof, and certainly the comprehender is greater than that which lieth within its grasp; for imagination is but the branch, while mind is the root; and certainly the root is greater than the branch . . . Thus are the people worshipping only *an error of perception*.
>
> But that Essence of Essences, that Invisible of Invisibles, is sanctified above all human speculation, and never to be overtaken by the mind of man. Never shall that immemorial Reality lodge within the compass of a contingent being. His is another realm, and of that realm no understanding can be won. No access can be gained thereto; all entry is forbidden there. *The utmost one can say is that Its existence can be proved, but the conditions of Its existence are unknown.* (emphasis added)[4]

Bahá'u'lláh also asserts that nothing can be said about God or Absolute Reality. Any description that we try to make of Him or It is completely inadequate:

> To every discerning and illuminated heart it is evident that God, the unknowable Essence, the Divine Being, is immensely exalted beyond every human attribute, such as corporeal existence, ascent and descent, egress and regress. Far be it from His glory that human tongue should adequately recount His praise, or that human heart comprehend His fathomless mystery. He is, and hath ever been, veiled in the ancient eternity of His Essence, and will remain in His Reality everlastingly hidden from the sight of men.[5]

Bahá'u'lláh says that the only connection that human beings have with this highest reality, the essence of God or the Absolute Reality, is through the prophet-founders of the world religions. These persons, although they appear in human form, are, in reality, intermediaries between the Absolute Reality/God and humanity. It is only through them that we can come to know anything at all about the highest reality:

> The door of the knowledge of the Ancient of Days being thus closed in the
> face of all beings, the Source of infinite grace . . . hath caused those
> luminous Gems of Holiness to appear out of the realm of the spirit, in the
> noble form of the human temple, and be made manifest unto all men, that
> they may impart unto the world the mysteries of the unchangeable Being,
> and tell of the subtleties of His imperishable Essence.[6]

Bahá'u'lláh does not, therefore, condemn the various concepts of God or
Absolute Reality held by the religions of East and West. He states that
they are true but are only limited and relative truths.

Regarding the Western concept of God described above, for
example, Bahá'u'lláh asserts that the Essence of God is 'beyond every
human attribute'.[7] Where the scriptures of the Western religions appear
to give God human attributes (such as being angry with one people and
being pleased with another; or coming and going; or speaking; or having
parts of the human body such as a face or hands or back), these are not
references to the Essence of God, the unknowable Godhead. In fact, all
these are references to the spiritual reality of the prophet-founders of the
world religions. Because these prophet-founders perfectly reflect all of
the names and attributes of God, Bahá'u'lláh calls them the
Manifestations of God. These exalted beings stand for God in this world:

> [God] hath ordained the knowledge of these sanctified Beings to be
> identical with the knowledge of His own Self. Whoso recognizeth them
> hath recognized God. Whoso hearkeneth to their call, hath hearkened to
> the Voice of God, and whoso testifieth to the truth of their Revelation,
> hath testified to the truth of God Himself. Whoso turneth away from
> them, hath turned away from God, and whoso disbelieveth in them, hath
> disbelieved in God . . . They are the Manifestations of God amidst men,
> the evidences of His Truth, and the signs of His glory.[8]

Since human beings can have no direct knowledge or understanding
of God, these Manifestations of God are all that human beings can know
of God in this world. All of the attributes of God recorded in the scriptures
can best be conceptualized through the person of these Manifestations:

> Viewed from the standpoint of their oneness and sublime detachment, the
> attributes of Godhead, Divinity, Supreme Singleness, and Inmost Essence,
> have been, and are applicable to those Essences of Being, inasmuch as they

all abide on the throne of Divine Revelation, and are established upon the seat of Divine Concealment. Through their appearance the Revelation of God is made manifest, and by their countenance the Beauty of God is revealed. Thus it is that the accents of God Himself have been heard uttered by these Manifestations of the Divine Being. (Bahá'u'lláh)[9]

With regard to the conceptualization of the Absolute Reality in the Eastern religions, Bahá'u'lláh again does not condemn this view. On the contrary, he affirms that it is in some senses true. For example he states that 'absolute existence is strictly confined to God,'[10] and nothing else can be said to exist in any absolute sense apart from God.[11]

Regarding the conceptualization in the Eastern religions of the Absolute Reality as identical with the human reality, Bahá'u'lláh makes many similar statements, for example: 'Turn thy sight unto thyself, that thou mayest find Me standing within thee, mighty, powerful and self-subsisting.'[12] Just as with the Western religious concepts of God, however, these statements hold true at the level of the manifestation of God. All of the divine names and attributes are manifested in the human being. In that sense, then, there is an identity between the human being and the Absolute, but it is an identity of attributes, not of essence.

In brief then, Bahá'u'lláh takes the concepts of both Eastern and Western religions and asserts that those who hold these views are both wrong and right. They are wrong if they maintain that these views are the absolute truth about the essence of the highest reality (for human beings have no access to that truth); but they are right in that these views do express the truth from a limited viewpoint (they represent the truth about the Absolute Reality/God in the way that it manifests itself in this world). This is all the truth that human beings can comprehend. The fact that the various expressions of this truth have been different and even sometimes contradictory is due to the limitations of the human mind and the fact that we are only able to view these truths from a particular limited viewpoint.

THE DIVINE EDUCATOR, THE MANIFESTATION OF GOD

In the natural order, all things need training and education to achieve their highest state of perfection. Cultivation can turn a desert area into a fruitful orchard or a wilderness into a beautiful garden. Human beings also need education and training. Left to themselves without an educator, they will grow up savage and bestial. The human spirit is in need of an educator too. The spiritual educators of humanity have been the prophet-founders of the world's religions. Baháʾuʾlláh says that the betterment of all things in the world depends upon the action of these divine educators.[13] ʿAbduʾl-Bahá asserts that these figures have not merely been great men; they could not have achieved what they did by human power alone.[14]

These divine educators and the religions that they establish have two roles: first, to enable human beings to progress spiritually as individuals; and second, to promote the peace and advancement of human civilization.

> God's purpose in sending His Prophets unto men is two-fold. The first is to liberate the children of men from the darkness of ignorance, and guide them to the light of true understanding. The second is to ensure the peace and tranquillity of mankind, and provide all the means by which they can be established. (Baháʾuʾlláh)[15]

As we have seen above (p. 94), Baháʾuʾlláh calls these divine educators the Manifestations of God. This is because they show forth (manifest) all of the divine names and attributes in a complete and perfect manner. The relation between God and the Manifestation of God is likened in the Baháʾí scriptures to a perfect mirror which reflects the light of the sun: 'All the perfections, the bounties, the splendours which come from God are visible and evident in the Reality of the Holy Manifestations, like the sun which is resplendent in a clear polished mirror with all its perfections and bounties' (ʿAbduʾl-Bahá).[16]

These Manifestations of God occupy a very exalted station. Since God is, for human beings, unknowable, the most that humans can know of God is through these figures, who are the perfect Manifestations of all the names and attributes of God. They are therefore 'as God' for human beings; it is the Manifestation 'Who representeth the Godhead in both the Kingdom of His Cause and the world of creation' (Baháʾuʾlláh).[17]

Since the founders of all the world religions are essentially the manifestations of one reality (see also p. 99), it follows that the religions themselves are fundamentally guiding human beings along one path – the path that will ensure their greatest spiritual progress.

Bahá'u'lláh has therefore urged the followers of the different religions to put aside their differences:

> The Great Being saith: O ye children of men! The fundamental purpose animating the Faith of God and His Religion is to safeguard the interests and promote the unity of the human race, and to foster the spirit of love and fellowship amongst men. Suffer it not to become a source of dissension and discord, of hate and enmity.[18]

Needless to say, Bahá'u'lláh has also urged his followers to enter into the spirit of religious reconciliation and harmony: 'Consort with the followers of all religions in a spirit of friendliness and fellowship. Whatsoever hath led the children of men to shun one another, and hath caused dissensions and divisions amongst them, hath, through the revelation of these words, been nullified and abolished.'[19] 'Abdu'l-Bahá expresses the same idea even more emphatically in his Will and Testament:

> Consort with all the peoples, kindreds and religions of the world with the utmost truthfulness, uprightness, faithfulness, kindliness, good-will and friendliness, that all the world of being may be filled with the holy ecstasy of the grace of Bahá, that ignorance, enmity, hate and rancour may vanish from the world and the darkness of estrangement amidst the peoples and kindreds of the world may give way to the Light of Unity. Should other peoples and nations be unfaithful to you show your fidelity unto them, should they be unjust toward you show justice towards them, should they keep aloof from you attract them to yourself, should they show their enmity be friendly towards them, should they poison your lives, sweeten their souls, should they inflict a wound upon you, be a salve to their sores. Such are the attributes of the sincere! Such are the attributes of the truthful![20]

TRUE RELIGION

In the opening passages of one of his most important books, the Book of Certitude (Kitáb-i-Íqán), Bahá'u'lláh states that those who wish to have faith and certainty in their lives must first free themselves from the things of this world: their ears from gossip; their minds from idle fancies; and their hearts from longing for the things of this world. He also asserts that the mysteries of the spiritual world will never be revealed to us until we cease to regard the words and actions of ordinary men and women as the standard by which to judge the spiritual world.

Failure to comply with the above conditions has prevented human beings from achieving spiritual growth and advancement. As examples of this, Bahá'u'lláh recalls the history of religion. He points to the fact that in each age, the people have longed for the coming of the saviour promised them in their holy books. And yet when a prophet does indeed come to them, they deny him, turn away from him, insult him and persecute his followers. All of the world's scriptures record such events.

Bahá'u'lláh states that the main reason for this rejection of the prophets was the close-mindedness and pride of the people and the fact that they were blindly following their religious leaders. If they had purified their hearts and judged fairly, they would not have opposed the divine educators of humankind. Instead, they relied on their own limited understandings of the holy scriptures, which they had learned from their religious leaders. And when they found the proofs brought forward by the new prophet to be different from these limited understandings, they arose in opposition to the prophet.

Bahá'u'lláh asserts that it has been the leaders of religion in every age who have held the people back from accepting the new prophet and benefiting from his teachings. It is these leaders who held the reins of authority in their grasp. Some of them were ignorant and did not understand the words of their own scriptures that foretold the coming of the new prophet. Others, through a desire to cling onto their leadership, led the people into error. It is they who gave the orders for the persecutions of the prophets and their followers. Thus it is that these religious leaders have been condemned in all the books of scripture.

Bahá'u'lláh gives the example of Jesus. All of the people of Israel rose up against Jesus when he came. They said that they knew of the Messiah prophesied in their scriptures, but he was going to fulfil the law of Moses. On the other hand, this young man from Nazareth, who claimed to be the Messiah, had caused the law of divorce and of the Sabbath, which were two important Judaic laws, to be broken. And what is more, none of the signs that were supposed to accompany the coming of the Messiah had been fulfilled; in particular, the Jews were expecting a Messiah who would lead them to victory over Rome and establish a Jewish state.

The same sequence of events, Bahá'u'lláh says, has occurred in each religion. The people failed to understand the real meaning of the words of their scriptures. Thus when they did not find the literal meaning of these words fulfilled, they rejected the prophets and persecuted them. They clung to their own false imaginings instead of asking the prophet himself to explain the real meaning of the scripture. Thus they deprived themselves of the benefits of the new divine teachings.

Bahá'u'lláh says that this is the true meaning of the Day of Judgement referred to in the scriptures of several religions. Whenever a new prophet appears, that is the 'end of the world' for the previous religious dispensation and a day of judgement for the followers of that religion: if they are sincere and faithful to the spirit of their religion, they recognize the new teaching from God; but if they are merely following the outward forms of their religion, they will be spiritually blind to the new teaching.

According to Bahá'u'lláh, the Manifestations of God are the successive appearances in the world of the same divine reality. They are therefore, in their essential nature, one:

> Inasmuch as these Birds of the Celestial Throne are all sent down from the heaven of the Will of God, and as they all arise to proclaim His irresistible Faith, they therefore are regarded as one soul and the same person. For they all drink from the one Cup of the love of God, and all partake of the fruit of the same Tree of Oneness.[21]

Bahá'u'lláh explains the differences among these Manifestations of God by asserting that they each have a twofold station. In their spiritual reality these prophet-founders of the world religions are one and the same. This is the 'station of pure abstraction and essential unity':

> In this respect, if thou callest them all by one name, and dost ascribe to them the same attribute, thou hast not erred from the truth . . . For they one and all summon the people of the earth to acknowledge the Unity of God . . . They are all invested with the robe of Prophethood, and honoured with the mantle of glory . . . Wherefore, should one of these

Manifestations of Holiness proclaim saying: 'I am the return of all the Prophets,' He verily speaketh the truth.[22]

The Manifestations of God differ, however, in their external aspects – their names, their bodily forms, the ages in which they came, and the specific messages that they brought. This is their second station, the 'station of distinction', which 'pertaineth to the world of creation and to the limitations thereof'.

> In this respect, each Manifestation of God hath a distinct individuality, a definitely prescribed mission, a predestined Revelation, and specially designated limitations. Each one of them is known by a different name, is characterized by a special attribute, fulfils a definite Mission, and is entrusted with a particular Revelation.[23]

Bahá'u'lláh gives the analogy of the sun. In order to mark the passing of time, human beings give each day a different name. If it were to be said that all the days are one and the same that would be true, for they are each the expression of the same reality, the appearance of the sun; and if it were to be said that, with regard to their names, they differ, that would also be true.[24] The oneness and differences of the prophets of God should be thought of in the same way. They are each the appearance on earth of the same reality, and thus are all one; and yet, relative to our human world, they each come at a different time and have a different name.

In view of their essential oneness, Bahá'u'lláh asserts that it would be wrong to prefer one of these prophet-founders of the world religions over another:

> Know thou assuredly that the essence of all the Prophets of God is one and the same. Their unity is absolute . . . To prefer one in honour to another, to exalt certain ones above the rest, is in no wise to be permitted. Every true Prophet hath regarded His Message as fundamentally the same as the Revelation of every other Prophet gone before Him. If any man, therefore, should fail to comprehend this truth, and should consequently indulge in vain and unseemly language, no one whose sight is keen and whose understanding is enlightened would ever allow such idle talk to cause him to waver in his belief.[25]

It is, however, the second station, that of distinctions and difference, that has confused humanity and made it appear that there are some inherent contradictions among the religions of the world:

> It is because of this difference in their station and mission that the words and utterances flowing from these Well-springs of divine knowledge appear to diverge and differ . . . As most of the people have failed to appreciate those stations to which We have referred, they therefore feel perplexed and dismayed at the varying utterances pronounced by Manifestations that are essentially one and the same. (Bahá'u'lláh)[26]

The differences among the teachings of the prophet-founders of the world religions arise because they have come to different parts of the world in which there are differing cultures. They therefore have to address their messages differently according to each culture. An even more important reason for difference is the fact that the needs of humanity have changed over the ages. The world now is very different from the world of one thousand or two thousand years ago, and so the message of God changes in accordance with this difference. The message of these Manifestations of God deals with the needs of the age in which they appear: 'For every age requireth a fresh measure of the light of God. Every Divine Revelation hath been sent down in a manner that befitted the circumstances of the age in which it hath appeared.'[27]

The successive prophets that have come to the earth have each taken humankind onwards in its social and spiritual evolution. They have helped humanity 'to carry forward an ever-advancing civilization'.[28] Each has built on the message of his predecessor and taken humanity on a further stage. This has been necessary because humanity is only able to advance a step at a time. Just as the rays of the sun at sunrise are weak and only gradually build up to their midday intensity otherwise they would cause great damage to all living things, so Bahá'u'lláh states that it would be injurious for a Manifestation of God to give a more advanced message than the one that he does in fact deliver.[29] The message that each of these prophet-founders of the world religions gives is in accordance with humanity's ability to receive it: 'All that I have revealed unto thee with the tongue of power, and have written for thee with the pen of might, hath been in accordance with thy capacity and understanding, not with My state and the melody of My voice' (Bahá'u'lláh).[30]

◆

THE DIVINE PHYSICIAN

The Prophets of God should be regarded as physicians whose task is to foster the well-being of the world and its peoples, that, through the spirit of oneness, they may heal the sickness of a divided humanity. To none is given the right to question their words or disparage their conduct, for they are the only ones who can claim to have understood the patient and to have correctly diagnosed its ailments . . . Little wonder, then, if the treatment prescribed by the physician in this day should not be found to be identical with that which he prescribed before. How could it be otherwise when the ills affecting the sufferer necessitate at every stage of his sickness a special remedy? In like manner, every time the Prophets of God have illumined the world . . . they have invariably summoned its peoples to embrace the light of God through such means as best befitted the exigencies of the age in which they appeared. They were thus able to scatter the darkness of ignorance, and to shed upon the world the glory of their own knowledge.

Bahá'u'lláh, *Gleanings,* no. 34, p. 80

◆

Bahá'u'lláh's own claim is that he is a Manifestation of God in the line of succession of the prophet-founders of the world religions. His mission is to take humanity on to the next stage of its development. The social and spiritual teachings that Bahá'u'lláh has brought are the teachings that he states will unite the world and bring about the fulfilment of the prophecies to be found in all of the religions of the world about a great day when there will be a golden age for humanity. Bahá'ís claim, therefore, that Bahá'u'lláh is the figure anticipated in the scriptures of all the religions of the world. He is the Everlasting Father and Prince of Peace foretold in the Hebrew Bible and expected by the Jews, the return of Christ in the glory of the Father awaited by Christians, the Great Announcement about which the Muslims are told in the Qur'án, the Shah Bahram of the Zoroastrian scriptures, the Kalki Avatar foretold in the Hindu scriptures, and the Maitreya Buddha that the Buddhists are awaiting.

In view of the teaching described above of the progressive revelation of truth through the successive Manifestations, Bahá'u'lláh does not regard himself as the final Manifestation of God. In due course, conditions will change again and a new divine message will become necessary. Bahá'u'lláh has written, however, that this will not occur for at least a thousand years.

Bahá'ís regard the Bahá'í Faith as an independent religion, alongside the other world religions, such as Christianity, Islam, Buddhism and Hinduism. Conversion to the Bahá'í Faith is not, however, similar to conversion to some other religions. When one converts from Christianity to Buddhism, for example, one rejects entirely the viewpoint that one is leaving behind and adopts a new viewpoint. Since the doctrines of the two religions appear to be contradictory, it is a question of adopting either one or the other. To become a Bahá'í, however, does not entail an automatic rejection of one's previous religion. In the first place, in view of the Bahá'í teaching that the prophet-founders of all of the world religions are the reappearance in the world of the same reality, conversion to the Bahá'í Faith involves no rejection of the founder of one's previous religion.

Second, from the Bahá'í viewpoint, to become a Bahá'í means that one has been faithful to the message of the founders of these religions in following their promise about the coming of a future saviour, a promise that Bahá'ís believe has been fulfilled by Bahá'u'lláh.

Third, humanity has over thousands of years developed numerous different viewpoints on religious questions; a multitude of diverse pathways to spirituality; many spiritual insights developed by the mystics and seers of the various religions. The Bahá'í Faith does not seek to reject or replace this rich religious heritage of humanity; rather, it seeks to preserve it, stripped of any divisive potential, within an overall framework of unity. Indeed, more than preserving this rich heritage, the Bahá'í Faith would seek to develop it and make it available globally, so that the best of every religion and culture can contribute to humanity's overall progress.

THE GOAL OF HUMAN LIFE (SALVATION)

The goal of human life is described in various ways in the Bahá'í scriptures. As we have seen in the first chapter, one way of expressing it is to say that our lives are an opportunity to fulfil our potential in being examples of the divine virtues and attributes. In order to do this, however, one must follow the teachings of one of the divine educators. Therefore Bahá'u'lláh states, as the opening verse of his major book, the Kitáb-i-Aqdas (the Most Holy Book), that the first duty for human beings is to recognize this divine educator, and the second is to follow his laws and teachings:

> The first duty prescribed by God for His servants is the recognition of Him Who is the Day Spring of His Revelation and the Fountain of His laws, Who representeth the Godhead in both the Kingdom of His Cause and the world of creation. Whoso achieveth this duty hath attained unto all good . . . It behoveth every one who reacheth this most sublime station . . . to observe every ordinance of Him Who is the Desire of the world. These twin duties are inseparable. Neither is acceptable without the other.[31]

If we are faithful to these two injunctions, then we will be following a path that involves a daily effort to develop spiritual qualities – an effort that is assisted by spiritual discipline, such as prayer. For human beings no other path can bring true happiness or lasting contentment: 'Wert thou to speed through the immensity of space and traverse the expanse of heaven, yet thou wouldst find no rest save in submission to Our command and humbleness before Our Face' (Bahá'u'lláh).[32]

This effort to develop spiritual qualities should not be seen as trying to become something different from what we already are; rather, it should be seen as releasing the divine potential that is already present in each person – for all human beings have the image of God engraved upon them:

> According to the words of the Old Testament God has said, 'Let us make man in our image, after our likeness.' This indicates that man is of the image and likeness of God – that is to say, the perfections of God, the divine virtues, are reflected or revealed in the human reality. ('Abdu'l-Bahá)[33]

Such spiritual processes are difficult to describe in words. There are, therefore, many metaphors and images used for this process in the Bahá'í scriptures. One is that of burnishing a mirror so that the divine sun shines in it with full glory:

> A pure heart is as a mirror; cleanse it with the burnish of love and

severance from all save God, that the true sun may shine within it and the eternal morning dawn. Then wilt thou clearly see the meaning of 'Neither doth My earth nor My heaven contain Me, but the heart of My faithful servant containeth Me.' (Bahá'u'lláh)[34]

Another image is that of a divine light within the human being: 'Thou art My lamp and My light is in thee. Get thou from it thy radiance and seek none other than Me. For I have created thee rich and have bountifully shed My favour upon thee' (Bahá'u'lláh).[35] The site within the human being of these spiritual qualities is described as the human heart. Unfortunately, it is too often also the site of love for the things of this world:

All that is in heaven and earth I have ordained for thee, except the human heart, which I have made the habitation of My beauty and glory; yet thou didst give My home and dwelling to another than Me; and whenever the manifestation of My holiness sought His own abode, a stranger found He there, and, homeless, hastened unto the sanctuary of the Beloved. Notwithstanding I have concealed thy secret and desired not thy shame. (Bahá'u'lláh)[36]

Thus human beings can either be turned towards the material world and have their hearts set on the appeasement of their animal nature – the state of being in sin as it is called in Christian terminology – or they can turn their hearts towards God and try to develop their spiritual nature. According to the Bahá'í scriptures, Satan or the Devil is the animal side of human nature. It is this animal side that constantly tempts us and keeps us from fulfilling our spiritual potential.

The divine potential within can, however, only be brought out if we have the will to proceed along the path mapped out by Bahá'u'lláh: 'All that which ye potentially possess can, however, be manifested only as a result of your own volition.'[37] We must aim to cleanse the human heart so that the Divine nature can manifest itself within us: 'Hast thou ever heard that friend and foe should abide in one heart? Cast out then the stranger, that the Friend may enter His home' (Bahá'u'lláh).[38] This is a process of sacrificing our earthly attachments in order to acquire spiritual characteristics (see p. 11). 'Abdu'l-Bahá likens it to placing an iron in the fire:

Man must become severed from the human world . . . the nether world become as non-existent and the Kingdom become manifest. He must become like unto the iron thrown within the furnace of fire. The qualities of iron, such as blackness, coldness and solidity which belong to the earth disappear and vanish while the characteristics of fire, such as redness, glowing and heat, which belong to the Kingdom become apparent and visible. Therefore, iron hath sacrificed its qualities and grades to the fire, acquiring the virtues of that element.[39]

Once the heart is cleansed in this way then the human being can turn towards the light at all times and under all circumstances:

In this station he pierceth the veils of plurality, fleeth from the worlds of the flesh, and ascendeth into the heaven of singleness. With the ear of God he heareth, with the eye of God he beholdeth the mysteries of divine creation . . . He seeth in himself neither name nor fame nor rank, but findeth his own praise in praising God . . . He looketh on all things with the eye of oneness, and seeth the brilliant rays of the divine sun shining from the dawning-point of Essence alike on all created things, and the lights of singleness reflected over all creation. (Bahá'u'lláh)[40]

If a person should succeed in achieving this state and of seeing with the eye of oneness, then the signs of the divine nature within will begin to show themselves. For that nature is within the individual but 'hidden under the veilings of sense and the conditions of this earth, even as a candle within a lantern of iron, and only when the lantern is removed doth the light of the candle shine out'.[41] And when that divine nature within begins to show itself, the person is transformed into a new entity:

Whensoever the light of Manifestation of the King of Oneness settleth upon the throne of the heart and soul, His shining becometh visible in every limb and member . . . For thus the Master of the house hath appeared within His home, and all the pillars of the dwelling are ashine with His light. And the action and effect of the light are from the Light-Giver; so it is that all move through Him and arise by His will. (Bahá'u'lláh)[42]

It is here that the human being reaches that contentment and inner peace for which we all long:

Pleasant is the realm of being, wert thou to attain thereto; glorious is the domain of eternity, shouldst thou pass beyond the world of mortality;

sweet is the holy ecstasy if thou drinkest of the mystic chalice from the hands of the celestial Youth. Shouldst thou attain this station, thou wouldst be freed from destruction and death, from toil and sin. (Bahá'u'lláh)[43]

In this spiritual world, everything is seen anew and the individual is lost in wonderment. Here the mystical traveller

is tossed in the oceans of grandeur, and at every moment his wonder groweth. Now he seeth the shape of wealth as poverty itself, and the essence of freedom as sheer impotence . . . At every moment he beholdeth a wondrous world, a new creation, and goeth from astonishment to astonishment, and is lost in awe at the works of the Lord of Oneness. (Bahá'u'lláh)[44]

◆

THE STATE OF CONTENTMENT

A master had a slave who was completely devoted to him. One day he gave the slave a melon which when cut open looked most ripe and delicious. The slave ate one piece, then another and another with great relish (the day being warm) until nearly the whole melon had disappeared. The master, picking up the last slice, tasted it, and found it exceedingly bitter and unpalatable. 'Why it is very bitter! Did you not find it so?' he asked the servant. 'Yes, my Master,' the slave replied, 'it was bitter and unpleasant, but I have tasted so much sweetness from thy hand that one bitter melon was not worth mentioning.'

Story told by 'Abdu'l-Bahá; Grundy,
Ten Days in the Light of 'Akká, p. 103

◆

The result is to achieve a station where the self of the individual vanishes completely allowing the divine nature it is concealing to shine out brightly. This is the station of true poverty and absolute nothingness:

This station is the dying from self and the living in God, the being poor in self and rich in the Desired One. Poverty as here referred to signifieth being poor in the things of the created world, rich in the things of God's world. For when the true lover and devoted friend reacheth to the presence of the Beloved, the sparkling beauty of the Loved One and the fire of the lover's heart will kindle a blaze and burn away all veils and wrappings. Yea, all he hath, from heart to skin, will be set aflame, so that nothing will remain save the Friend. (Bahá'u'lláh)[45]

THE CAUSE AND PURPOSE OF SUFFERING

During our lives we inevitably have periods of time when things are not going well. Whether it be caused by death, poverty, disease or the actions of others, suffering is an inevitable consequence of our lives on this earth. There are periods when nothing seems to go right and every path to happiness is blocked with insurmountable barriers. Alternatively, we may be struck by suffering on a huge scale caused by a war or a natural disaster.

Some of our suffering is, of course, the direct result of our own actions: something that we have done wrong or unwisely. The Bahá'í teachings assert that the universe is governed by physical, moral and spiritual laws, if we break or go against these laws, we must expect to suffer the consequences. Thus someone who flouts the physical laws in the world and walks in front of a moving car must expect to get hurt; similarly, if we go against the moral laws and act dishonestly, for example, we should not be surprised if we are punished when this is found out; and if we go against the spiritual laws of the universe and fail to pray or to detach ourselves from the physical things of this world, for example, then we must expect to be unhappy and feel discontented.

Our suffering is not, however, always caused by something that we have done. It is often at such times that we start to wonder about the reason for suffering. The possibility that a loving God would allow such suffering is frequently questioned.

Bahá'u'lláh says that the whole of this world that we see before us has been created by God for the education and spiritual development of human beings:

> Out of the wastes of nothingness, with the clay of My command I made thee to appear, and have ordained for thy training every atom in existence and the essence of all created things. Thus, ere thou didst issue from thy mother's womb, I destined for thee two founts of gleaming milk, eyes to watch over thee, and hearts to love thee. Out of My loving-kindness, 'neath the shade of My mercy I nurtured thee, and guarded thee by the essence of My grace and favour. And My purpose in all this was that thou mightest attain My everlasting dominion and become worthy of My invisible bestowals.[46]

THE MEANING OF SUFFERING

In October 1913, 'Abdu'l-Bahá was in California. There he visited a black Bahá'í, Charles Tinsley, who was laid up in bed with a broken leg. Tinsley expressed to 'Abdu'l-Bahá his frustration with his situation and voiced a desire to be up and about, teaching the Bahá'í Faith to others. 'Abdu'l-Bahá is reported to have replied:

You must not be sad. This affliction will make you spiritually stronger. Do not be sad. Cheer up! Praise be to God, you are dear to me. I will tell you a story: A certain ruler wished to appoint one of his subjects to a high office; so, in order to train him, the ruler cast him into prison and caused him to suffer much. The man was surprised at this, for he expected great favours. The ruler had him taken from prison and beaten with sticks. This greatly astonished the man, for he thought the ruler loved him. After this he was hanged on the gallows until he was nearly dead. After he recovered he asked the ruler, 'If you love me, why did you do these things?' The ruler replied: 'I wish to make you prime minister. By having gone through these ordeals you are better fitted for that office. I wish you to know how it is yourself. When you are obliged to punish, you will know how it feels to endure these things. I love you so I wish you to become perfect.'

[To Mr Tinsley] Even so with you. After this ordeal you will reach maturity. God sometimes causes us to suffer much and to have many misfortunes that we may become strong in his Cause.

You will recover and be spiritually stronger than ever before. You will work for God and carry the Message to many of your people.

Star of the West, vol. 4, 1913, no. 12, p. 205

Since the whole of creation is for the express purpose of promoting the spiritual welfare of human beings, it is not surprising to find that the Bahá'í teachings assert that suffering is also sometimes caused by God for this purpose. Pain, as we have seen (see p. 12), is an inevitable part of detaching ourselves from the attractions of this physical world. When 'Abdu'l-Bahá was asked: 'Does the soul progress more through sorrow or through the joy in this world?' he replied:

The mind and spirit of man advance when he is tried by suffering. The more the ground is ploughed the better the seed will grow, the better the harvest will be. Just as the plough furrows the earth deeply, purifying it of weeds and thistles, so suffering and tribulation free man from the petty affairs of this worldly life until he arrives at a state of complete detachment. His attitude in this world will be that of divine happiness. Man is, so to speak, unripe: the heat of the fire of suffering will mature him. Look back to the times past and you will find that the greatest men have suffered most . . .

To attain eternal happiness one must suffer. He who has reached the state of self-sacrifice has true joy. Temporal joy will vanish.[47]

For this reason Bahá'u'lláh even calls upon us to welcome suffering as an opportunity for our spiritual development: 'My calamity is My providence, outwardly it is fire and vengeance, but inwardly it is light and mercy. Hasten thereunto that thou mayest become an eternal light and an immortal spirit. This is My command unto thee, do thou observe it.'[48]

This does not, however, answer all of the questions regarding suffering. What of those who die and have no chance to develop through their suffering? What of the suffering of small children?

As to the subject of babes and infants and weak ones who are afflicted by the hands of oppressors: This contains great wisdom and this subject is of paramount importance. In brief, for those souls there is a recompense in another world and many details are connected with this matter. For those souls that suffering is the greatest mercy of God. Verily that mercy of the Lord is far better and preferable to all the comfort of this world and the growth and development of this place of mortality.[49]

LIFE AFTER DEATH

The Bahá'í scriptures affirm the existence of an eternal soul connected with each human being, although we cannot really understand its nature: 'Thou hast asked Me concerning the nature of the soul. Know, verily, that the soul is a sign of God, a heavenly gem whose reality the most learned of men hath failed to grasp, and whose mystery no mind, however acute, can ever hope to unravel' (Bahá'u'lláh).[50] The soul cannot be said, however, to reside within the body:

The rational soul, meaning the human spirit, does not descend into the body – that is to say, it does not enter it, for descent and entrance are characteristics of bodies, and the rational soul is exempt from this. The spirit never entered this body, so in quitting it, it will not be in need of an abiding-place: no, the spirit is connected with the body, as this light is with this mirror. ('Abdu'l-Bahá)[51]

Our life, therefore, does not end with our death: 'To consider that after the death of the body the spirit perishes is like imagining that a bird in a cage will be destroyed if the cage is broken, though the bird has nothing to fear from the destruction of the cage' ('Abdu'l-Bahá).[52]

The Bahá'í Faith teaches that the spiritual reality of the human being, the human soul, continues eternally. It passes on to another plane of existence. To describe that world, however, is difficult:

> The world beyond is as different from this world as this world is different from that of the child while still in the womb of its mother. When the soul attaineth the Presence of God, it will assume the form that best befitteth its immortality and is worthy of its celestial habitation. (Bahá'u'lláh)[53]

To carry the analogy further, just as it is necessary for the embryo in the womb to prepare itself for this life, so we must prepare ourselves for the next world:

> In the beginning of his human life man was embryonic in the world of the matrix. There he received capacity and endowment for the reality of human existence. The forces and powers necessary for this world were bestowed upon him in that limited condition. In this world he needed eyes; he received them potentially in the other. He needed ears; he obtained them there in readiness and preparation for his new existence . . .
>
> Therefore, in this world he must prepare himself for the life beyond. That which he needs in the world of the Kingdom must be obtained here. Just as he prepared himself in the world of the matrix by acquiring forces necessary in this sphere of existence, so, likewise, the indispensable forces of the divine existence must be potentially attained in this world. ('Abdu'l-Bahá)[54]

And so, rather than trying to understand the next world, something that no human being will ever truly achieve, the individual should be concerned with the question of what must be gained in this world in order to be complete and fulfilled in the next.

> That world beyond is a world of sanctity and radiance; therefore, it is necessary that in this world he should acquire these divine attributes. In that world there is need of spirituality, faith, assurance, the knowledge and love of God. These he must attain in this world so that after his ascension from the earthly to the heavenly Kingdom he shall find all that is needful in that eternal life ready for him.

THE SOUL AFTER DEATH

And now concerning thy question regarding the soul of man and its survival after death. Know thou of a truth that the soul, after its separation from the body, will continue to progress until it attaineth the presence of God, in a state and condition which neither the revolution of ages and centuries, nor the changes and chances of this world, can alter. It will endure as long as the Kingdom of God, His sovereignty, His dominion and power will endure. It will manifest the signs of God and His attributes, and will reveal His loving kindness and bounty. The movement of My Pen is stilled when it attempteth to befittingly describe the loftiness and glory of so exalted a station. The honour with which the Hand of Mercy will invest the soul is such as no tongue can adequately reveal, nor any other earthly agency describe.

Blessed is the soul which, at the hour of its separation from the body, is sanctified from the vain imaginings of the peoples of the world. Such a soul liveth and moveth in accordance with the Will of its Creator, and entereth the all-highest Paradise. The Maids of Heaven, inmates of the loftiest mansions, will circle around it, and the Prophets of God and His chosen ones will seek its companionship. With them that soul will freely converse, and will recount unto them that which it hath been made to endure in the path of God, the Lord of all worlds. If any man be told that which hath been ordained for such a soul in the worlds of God, the Lord of the throne on high and of earth below, his whole being will instantly blaze out in his great longing to attain that most exalted, that sanctified and resplendent station ...

The nature of the soul after death can never be described, nor is it meet and permissible to reveal its whole character to the eyes of men. The Prophets and Messengers of God have been sent down for the sole purpose of guiding mankind to the straight Path of Truth. The purpose underlying Their revelation hath been to educate all men, that they may, at the hour of death, ascend, in the utmost purity and sanctity and with absolute detachment, to the throne of the Most High. The light which these souls radiate is responsible for the progress of the world and the advancement of its peoples. They are like unto leaven which leaveneth the world of being, and constitute the animating force through which the arts and wonders of the world are made manifest. Through them the clouds rain their bounty upon men, and the earth bringeth forth its fruits. All things must needs have a cause, a motive power, an animating principle. These souls and symbols of detachment have provided, and will continue to provide, the supreme moving impulse in the world of being.

The world beyond is as different from this world as this world is different from that of the child while still in the womb of its mother. When the soul attaineth the Presence of God, it will assume the form that best befitteth its immortality and is worthy of its celestial habitation.

Bahá'u'lláh, *Gleanings*, no. 81, pp. 155–7

That divine world is manifestly a world of lights; therefore, man has need of illumination here. That is a world of love; the love of God is essential. It is a world of perfections; virtues, or perfections, must be acquired. That world is vivified by the breaths of the Holy Spirit; in this world we must seek them. That is the Kingdom of everlasting life; it must be attained during this vanishing existence.[55]

The means of acquiring these virtues and characteristics are enumerated by 'Abdu'l-Bahá:

By what means can man acquire these things? How shall he obtain these merciful gifts and powers? First, through the knowledge of God. Second, through the love of God. Third, through faith. Fourth, through philanthropic deeds. Fifth, through self-sacrifice. Sixth, through severance from this world. Seventh, through sanctity and holiness. Unless he acquires these forces and attains to these requirements, he will surely be deprived of the life that is eternal. But if he possesses the knowledge of God, becomes ignited through the fire of the love of God, witnesses the great and mighty signs of the Kingdom, becomes the cause of love among mankind and lives in the utmost state of sanctity and holiness, he shall surely attain to second birth, be baptized by the Holy Spirit and enjoy everlasting existence.[56]

'Abdu'l-Bahá goes on in this same passage to lament the fact that so few human beings fulfil this all-important purpose of their lives:

Is it not astonishing that although man has been created for the knowledge and love of God, for the virtues of the human world, for spirituality, heavenly illumination and eternal life, nevertheless, he continues ignorant and negligent of all this? Consider how he seeks knowledge of everything except knowledge of God . . . He puts forth arduous labours to fathom terrestrial mysteries but is not at all concerned about knowing the mysteries of the Kingdom, traversing the illimitable fields of the eternal world, becoming informed of the divine realities, discovering the secrets of God, attaining the knowledge of God, witnessing the splendours of the Sun of Truth and realizing the glories of everlasting life. He is unmindful and thoughtless of these.[57]

Bahá'ís believe that those who have followed the teachings of the prophets and have developed their spiritual aspect will find the benefits of what they have done after death:

Thou hast, moreover, asked Me concerning the state of the soul after its separation from the body. Know thou, of a truth, that if the soul of man hath walked in the ways of God, it will, assuredly, return and be gathered to the glory of the Beloved. By the righteousness of God! It shall attain a station such as no pen can depict, or tongue describe. The soul that hath remained faithful to the Cause of God, and stood unwaveringly firm in His Path shall, after his ascension, be possessed of such power that all the worlds which the Almighty hath created can benefit through him. (Bahá'u'lláh)[58]

There can be no irrefutable proof of life after death. In several places, however, Bahá'u'lláh gives the phenomenon of dreams as evidence of the existence of worlds other than this world:

Verily I say, the human soul is exalted above all egress and regress. It is still, and yet it soareth; it moveth, and yet it is still. It is, in itself, a testimony that beareth witness to the existence of a world that is contingent, as well as to the reality of a world that hath neither beginning nor end. Behold how the dream thou hast dreamed is, after the lapse of many years, re-enacted before thine eyes. Consider how strange is the mystery of the world that appeareth to thee in thy dream. Ponder in thine heart upon the unsearchable wisdom of God, and meditate on its manifold revelations.[59]

One particular teaching of the Bahá'í Faith is that one can either perform good deeds or say prayers of intercession on behalf of those who have died, in order to assist their progress in the next world:

The progress of man's spirit in the divine world, after the severance of its connection with the body of dust, is through the bounty and grace of the Lord alone, or through the intercession and the sincere prayers of other human souls, or through the charities and important good works which are performed in its name. ('Abdu'l-Bahá)[60]

◆

PRAYER OF INTERCESSION FOR THE DEAD

O my God! O Thou forgiver of sins, bestower of gifts, dispeller of afflictions!
　　Verily, I beseech Thee to forgive the sins of such as have abandoned the physical garment and have ascended to the spiritual world.
　　O my Lord! Purify them from trespasses, dispel their sorrows, and change their darkness into light. Cause them to enter the garden of happiness, cleanse them with the most pure water, and grant them to behold Thy splendours on the loftiest mount.

'Abdu'l-Bahá, *Bahá'í Prayers*, pp. 45–6

◆

---

8 THE HISTORY OF THE BAHÁ'Í FAITH

In the course of a little more than 150 years, the Bahá'í Faith has grown from an obscure movement within a minority sect of Islam into a worldwide religion. In an introductory book such as this, only the briefest outline of its history can be given.

THE BÁB

The origins of the Bahá'í Faith go back to a religious movement founded in ad 1844 by a young Iranian merchant, Sayyid 'Alí Muḥammad Shírází, who took the title of the Báb (the gate). His followers were therefore called Bábís. In 1844, the Báb gathered around himself in the southern Iranian city of Shiraz a group of eighteen disciples whom he named the 'Letters of the Living'. Among these disciples was one woman, who was given the title of Ṭáhirih (the pure one). She was not in Shiraz but the Báb accepted her as one of the Letters of the Living on account of a message of acceptance that she sent him. These disciples the Báb dispersed throughout Iran and surrounding countries to spread his message, while he himself set off towards the end of 1844 on the pilgrimage to Mecca.

In Islam, there is the expectation of the coming of a messianic figure called the Mahdi. Among the Shí'í Muslims who predominate in Iran, it is believed that the Mahdi is the twelfth of a series of religious leaders, called Imams, who lived in the seventh to ninth centuries ad. The twelfth Imam is thought to have gone into hiding (occultation) in the ninth century and Shí'í Muslims are awaiting his return as the Mahdi. Initially, many people thought that the Báb was claiming to be the gateway to the hidden Imam Mahdi. Those who were religious scholars soon realized, however, from his writings, that the Báb was in fact claiming a far higher station. He was claiming to be in receipt of a divine revelation that would place him on a par with Muhammad, the founder of Islam. The Báb was proclaiming the start of a new religious cycle.

In Mecca, the Báb announced his message, but was generally ignored. His plans for proceeding from Mecca to Karbala, a holy city in the south of Iraq, also came to nothing owing to the fierce opposition that one of his disciples had encountered there. The Báb returned to Shiraz and was detained and placed under house arrest by the governor of that city.

Despite these early setbacks, the message of the Báb spread throughout Iran. Many thousands of people became his followers, including many religious scholars of Islam. The governor of Shiraz, fearing the growth of the movement, decided to arrest the Báb again in 1846. His officials carried out the arrest, but the sudden appearance of cholera in the city threw everything into confusion and the Báb was allowed to leave the city. He journeyed to the city of Isfahan in central Iran. The governor of Isfahan was a Georgian Christian who had converted to Islam and risen to his present high position. He asked the leading Shí'í religious official in the city to accommodate the Báb.

Isfahan was then the leading centre of Shí'í Islam in Iran. There the Báb wrote several of his most important works and discussed these with the religious scholars and students gathered there. His teachings convinced many, including the governor of Isfahan. The latter offered to put his personal fortune at the disposal of the Báb and to arrange a personal interview with the Shah.

Reports from Isfahan and all over Iran were arriving at the capital about the new religious movement. They alarmed the prime minister, who sent orders to Isfahan for the arrest of the Báb. The governor of Isfahan hid the Báb for a time in one of his palaces, but in February 1847, this governor died. His successor had the Báb sent under guard towards Tehran.

The prime minister, whose own position was dependent on the religious influence that he wielded over the Shah, feared that a meeting between the Báb and the Shah would lead to the loss of his own position.

He therefore halted the progress of the Báb's escort outside Tehran and diverted them to Maku in the extreme north-west of Iran. The prime minister hoped that, here in a remote corner of the country and imprisoned among a hostile people, the Báb would be isolated and his movement would gradually die away.

The prime minister's hopes were not, however, fulfilled. The Báb won over his prison warder in Maku, and his teachings continued to spread through the towns and villages of Iran. In 1848, several significant events occurred. Early in that year, the prime minister changed the Báb's place of imprisonment from Maku to Chihriq in the hope of making him more isolated. Also in that year, the Báb issued the Bayán, his principal book of laws and teachings. This book made it clear that he was in fact inaugurating a new religious dispensation which abrogated the dispensation of Islam. This fact was then proclaimed in a conference of his followers held in the summer of that year in a village called Badasht on the road between Tehran and the north-east. At about the same time, the prime minister had the Báb brought from his imprisonment to Tabriz, the provincial capital of the north-west. There a mock trial was held before the crown prince and an assembly of religious notables, in the hope that the Báb would be humiliated. The Báb, however, conducted himself with a dignity that won him even more supporters. The trial also gave the Báb an opportunity to announce publicly his claim to be the Mahdi of Islam.

In the autumn of 1848 a group of Bábís set out from the north-east religious centre of Mashad to rescue the Báb. These followers of the Báb proceeded westwards, skirting the southern coast of the Caspian Sea, but were held up at a religious shrine called Shaykh Tabarsi, some 100 miles north-east of Tehran. The old Shah had just died and his prime minister had been driven out of office. The new Shah was a young man and, together with his new prime minister, decided to act vigorously against the Bábís. They sent several regiments of troops with artillery to besiege the Bábís in Shaykh Tabarsi. The Bábís were, for the most part, religious scholars and other ordinary people numbering a few hundred, and were besieged in a place with no natural fortifications. Despite these disadvantages, they resisted the efforts of the Shah's army and even gained several notable victories over them. Eventually, in May 1849, after a seven-month siege, the Shah's commander was forced to resort to treachery to overcome the Bábís. After swearing an oath on the Qurʼán that he would grant them safe passage, he broke his word and attacked them when they emerged from their positions. Several leading Bábís died in that episode.

From this time on, the new Shah and his prime minister pursued an aggressive policy of suppressing the Bábís. There were two towns where the Bábís formed a significant proportion of the population: Zanjan (in the north-west on the road between Tehran and Tabriz) and Nayriz (in the south of the country, not far from Shiraz). Here the general climate of persecution forced the Bábís to take up defensive positions in 1850. After sieges by the royal troops, lasting two months in the case of Nayriz and eight months in the case of Zanjan, the Bábís were once more overcome and massacred.

In the middle of 1850, the prime minister decided that the only way of stopping the religious movement would be to execute the founder. He therefore had the Báb brought to Tabriz again and suspended in a public square in front of a firing squad consisting of a regiment of soldiers. There then occurred what Baháʼís consider to have been a miracle: all of the shots missed, and the Báb seemed to have disappeared. He was eventually found dictating his last words to his secretary. The Báb was then brought back to the square, suspended again, and a new regiment was lined up (the first regiment having refused to carry out a further attempt). This time they succeeded and the Báb was killed. His body was rescued by some of his followers. After being hidden in various places for almost sixty years, it was eventually interred in a shrine on the slopes of Mount Carmel in the city of Haifa. An imposing superstructure was then built over this shrine (see p. 72).

The persecution of the Bábís continued over the next few years. Eventually, in the summer of 1852, a small group of Bábís decided to obtain revenge on the Shah by assassinating him. Their plans were, however, poorly made and the plot was a failure. Although most Bábís had not been involved in the plot, this event triggered an intense persecution that resulted in the execution of almost all of the remaining leading Bábís. Among those executed was Ṭáhirih, the female member of the Letters of the Living.

BAHÁ'U'LLÁH

Bahá'u'lláh, the founder of the Bahá'í Faith, is the title taken by Mírzá Husayn 'Alí Núrí, the son of a prominent Iranian nobleman. He was born in Tehran on 12 November 1817. In the first year of the Báb's mission, 1844, Bahá'u'lláh (translated as 'The Glory of God') became an enthusiastic supporter of the new teachings. His home in Tehran became an important headquarters of the movement. When the Bábís began to be persecuted Bahá'u'lláh also suffered, and was arrested several times and beaten. Although he had been in no way involved in the attempted assassination of the Shah in 1852, Bahá'u'lláh was arrested and thrown into an underground pit called the Siyah Chal.

It was while he was in this pit that he had a visionary experience which he describes thus:

> While engulfed in tribulations I heard a most wondrous, a most sweet voice, calling above My head. Turning My face, I beheld a Maiden – the embodiment of the remembrance of the name of My Lord – suspended in the air before Me. So rejoiced was she in her very soul that her countenance shone with the ornament of the good-pleasure of God, and her cheeks glowed with the brightness of the All-Merciful. Betwixt earth and heaven she was raising a call which captivated the hearts and minds of men. She was imparting to both My inward and outer being tidings which rejoiced My soul, and the souls of God's honoured servants. Pointing with her finger unto My head, she addressed all who are in heaven and all who are on earth, saying: 'By God! This is the Best-Beloved of the worlds, and yet ye comprehend not. This is the Beauty of God amongst you, and the power of His sovereignty within you, could ye but understand. This is the Mystery of God and His Treasure, the Cause of God and His glory unto all who are in the kingdoms of Revelation and of creation, if ye be of them that perceive.'[1]

In the Bahá'í Faith, this episode is seen as equivalent to the Burning Bush in the Mosaic dispensation, to the Dove that descended upon Jesus after his baptism by John the Baptist, to the enlightenment of the Buddha under the Bo tree, and to the first appearance of the Angel Gabriel to Muhammad.

Although most of the Bábí prisoners in the Siyah Chal were executed, Bahá'u'lláh's life was spared because of his high social position and the intervention of the Russian minister in Tehran (Bahá'u'lláh's sister was married to an official of the Russian legation). Bahá'u'lláh was released from imprisonment on the condition that he go into exile. Although the Russian minister offered him the choice of proceeding to Russian territory, Bahá'u'lláh preferred to go to Baghdad (no doubt foreseeing that, if he went to Russia, he would become a pawn in the political game that was being played between Russia and England for supremacy in Iran).

In Baghdad, Bahá'u'lláh proceeded to revitalize the Bábí community. The Bábís had become demoralized and degraded as a result of the persecutions that had decimated their ranks. For two years, 1854–6, he withdrew to the mountains of Kurdistan. For part of this time he lived alone; the rest of the time he was a guest in a Sufi retreat in the town of Sulaymaniyya. Here he expounded on mystical themes and many people came to hear him. When he returned to Baghdad at the end of this time, he kept his contacts with some of these Sufis. His two main mystical works, the Seven Valleys and the Four Valleys, were written to two Sufi leaders. While in Baghdad, Bahá'u'lláh wrote several other important works. These included the Hidden Words, a series of aphorisms on spiritual and ethical themes, and the Book of Certitude (Kitáb-i-Íqán), which deals with the nature of religion and explains the fulfilment in the present day of the prophecies of the holy books of the past.

The Iranian authorities made representations to the Ottoman government about the presence and increasing influence of Bahá'u'lláh in Baghdad, close to the Iranian border. Orders eventually came that Bahá'u'lláh was to go to Istanbul, the capital of the Ottoman Empire. In many places in his writings, the Báb had written of a Messianic figure whom he called 'Him whom God shall make manifest'. Just before his departure from Baghdad in April 1863, Bahá'u'lláh announced to a group of his Bábí companions his claim to be the one promised by the Báb (this event is commemorated by Bahá'ís each year in the holy days of Riḍván; see p. 74).

Bahá'u'lláh remained in Istanbul for only three months before being sent on to Edirne (Adrianople) in European Turkey. Here Bahá'u'lláh openly announced his claim to be the one foretold by the Báb and the inaugurator of a new religious dispensation. He sent his emissaries to Iran to publicize this claim among the Bábís, almost all of whom now became Bahá'ís. While in Edirne, Bahá'u'lláh also began a series of letters that he sent to the leading monarchs of his time. He called on them to turn to his teachings, to abandon warfare, and become reconciled among themselves. He also wrote to the Muslim and Christian religious leaders, informing them of his claim to be the one promised in their scriptures.

In Edirne, Bahá'u'lláh experienced opposition from his half-brother, Mírzá Yaḥyá Azal. Azal had been promoted by the Báb to be a figurehead among the Bábís. After the execution of the Báb, many had looked to him to be the leader of the Bábís. Azal, however, was not a capable leader. Many Bábís were, therefore, already looking to Bahá'u'lláh for leadership even before he had put forward his claim. Azal did manage, however, to cause Bahá'u'lláh many problems. He attempted to kill Bahá'u'lláh by poisoning and the result caused Bahá'u'lláh's hand to shake for the rest of his life. Azal also sent inflammatory reports to the Ottoman authorities, the result of which was to cause them to send both Azal and Bahá'u'lláh off into further exile. This opposition from Azal is similar to the opposition experienced by other Manifestations of God from those close to them; the injury caused to Jesus by one of his twelve disciples, Judas Iscariot, and the opposition to the Buddha from his cousin Devadatta, for example.

EXTRACTS FROM BAHÁ'U'LLÁH'S TABLETS TO THE KINGS AND RELIGIOUS LEADERS

TO QUEEN VICTORIA

O Queen in London! Incline thine ear unto the voice of thy Lord, the Lord of all mankind, calling from the Divine Lote-Tree: Verily, no God is there but Me, the Almighty, the All-Wise! Cast away all that is on earth, and attire the head of thy kingdom with the crown of the remembrance of thy Lord, the All-Glorious. He, in truth, hath come unto the world in His most great glory, and all that hath been mentioned in the Gospel hath been fulfilled . . .

We have been informed that thou hast forbidden the trading in slaves, both men and women. This, verily, is what God hath enjoined in this wondrous Revelation. God hath, truly, destined a reward for thee, because of this. He, verily, will pay the doer of good his due recompense, wert thou to follow what hath been sent unto thee by Him Who is the All-Knowing, the All-Informed. As to him who turneth aside, and swelleth with pride, after that the clear tokens have come unto him, from the Revealer of signs, his work shall God bring to naught . . .

We have also heard that thou hast entrusted the reins of counsel into the hands of the representatives of the people. Thou, indeed, hast done well, for thereby the foundations of the edifice of thine affairs will be strengthened, and the hearts of all that are beneath thy shadow, whether high or low, will be tranquillized. It behoveth them, however, to be trustworthy among His servants, and to regard themselves as the representatives of all that dwell on earth. This is what counselleth them, in this Tablet, He Who is the Ruler, the All-Wise . . . Blessed is he that entereth the assembly for the sake of God, and judgeth between men with pure justice.

Bahá'u'lláh, *Proclamation of Bahá'u'lláh*, pp. 31–5

TO POPE PIUS IX

O Pope! Rend the veils asunder. He Who is the Lord of Lords is come overshadowed with clouds, and the decree hath been fulfilled by God, the Almighty, the Unrestrained . . . He, verily, hath again come down from Heaven even as He came down from it the first time. Beware that thou dispute not with Him even as the Pharisees disputed with Him (Jesus) without a clear token or proof. On His right hand flow the living waters of grace, and on His left the choice Wine of justice, whilst before Him march the angels of Paradise, bearing the banners of His signs. Beware lest any name debar thee from God, the Creator of earth and heaven. Leave thou the world behind thee, and turn towards thy Lord, through Whom the whole earth hath been illumined . . . Dwellest thou in palaces whilst He Who is the King of Revelation liveth in the most desolate of abodes? Leave them unto such as desire them, and set thy face with joy and delight towards the Kingdom . . . Arise in the name of thy Lord, the God of Mercy, amidst the peoples of the earth, and seize thou the Cup of Life with the hands of confidence, and first drink thou therefrom, and proffer it then to such as turn towards it amongst the peoples of all faiths . . .

Call thou to remembrance Him Who was the Spirit (Jesus), Who when He came, the most learned of His age pronounced judgment against Him in His own country, whilst he who was only a fisherman believed in Him. Take heed, then, ye men of understanding heart! Thou, in truth, art one of the suns of the heaven of His names. Guard thyself, lest darkness spread its veils over thee, and fold thee away from His light . . . Consider those who opposed the Son (Jesus), when He came unto them with sovereignty and power. How many the Pharisees who were waiting to behold Him, and were lamenting over their separation from Him! And yet, when the fragrance of His coming was wafted over them, and His beauty was unveiled, they turned aside from Him and disputed with Him . . . None save a very few, who were destitute of any power amongst men, turned towards His face. And yet, today, every man endowed with power and invested with sovereignty prideth himself on His

Name! In like manner, consider how numerous, in these days, are the monks who, in My Name, have secluded themselves in their churches, and who, when the appointed time was fulfilled, and We unveiled Our beauty, knew Us not, though they call upon Me at eventide and at dawn. . .

The Word which the Son concealed is made manifest. It hath been sent down in the form of the human temple in this day. Blessed be the Lord Who is the Father! He, verily, is come unto the nations in His most great majesty. Turn your faces towards Him, O concourse of the righteous. . . This is the day whereon the Rock (Peter) crieth out and shouteth, and celebrateth the praise of its Lord, the All-Possessing, the Most High, saying: 'Lo! The Father is come, and that which ye were promised in the Kingdom is fulfilled! . . .' My body longeth for the cross, and Mine head waiteth the thrust of the spear, in the path of the All-Merciful, that the world may be purged from its transgressions.

Bahá'u'lláh, *Proclamation of Bahá'u'lláh*, pp. 83–6

◆

In 1867, orders came that Bahá'u'lláh and his companions were to leave Edirne. Without knowing where they were going, they were forced to sell their possessions and leave. They were taken to Gallipoli and put aboard a ship. Eventually they arrived in the prison-city of Akka in Palestine (Azal was sent to Cyprus where he remained until his death).

In Akka, Bahá'u'lláh was at first imprisoned in the citadel for two years. When that building was required for other purposes, he was placed in a succession of houses in the city under house arrest. Soldiers guarded the city gate with strict instructions not to let Bahá'u'lláh or his companions out or to let any of his followers who came to meet him into the city. It was in these circumstances that Bahá'u'lláh wrote his most important book, the Kitáb-i-Aqdas (the Most Holy Book), in which he outlined his main religious laws. This was followed in the next two decades by a series of writings (tablets as they are called by Bahá'ís) in which he gave the distinctive teachings of his religious dispensation.

The personality of Bahá'u'lláh and the character of his companions eventually overcame the hostility of the authorities. In 1877, Bahá'u'lláh was allowed to move outside the city walls. In 1879, he took up residence in the mansion of Bahjí just outside Akka.

The last years of Bahá'u'lláh's life were spent in writing and dictating numerous works; receiving the pilgrims that came in increasing numbers; and directing the affairs of his religion. The religion itself was now gradually spreading into Egypt, Anatolia, the Caucasus, Central Asia and India. Even in Iran, despite episodes of persecution from time to time, the Bahá'í Faith was spreading among all classes and in all parts of the country.

◆

PEN-PORTRAIT OF BAHÁ'U'LLÁH

One of the few Westerners to meet Bahá'u'lláh was Professor Edward G. Browne, an orientalist from Cambridge University. He has left this description of his meeting with Bahá'u'lláh:

My conductor paused for a moment while I removed my shoes. Then, with a quick movement of the hand, he withdrew, and, as I passed replaced the curtain; and I found myself in a large apartment, along the upper end of which ran a low divan, while on the side opposite to the door were placed two or three chairs. Though I dimly suspected whither I was going and whom I was to behold (for no distinct intimation had been given to me), a second or two elapsed ere, with a throb of wonder and awe, I became definitely conscious that the room was not untenanted. In the corner where the divan met the wall sat a wondrous and venerable figure, crowned with a felt head-dress of the kind called táj by dervishes (but of unusual height and make), round the base of which was wound a small white turban. The face of him on whom I gazed I can never forget, though I cannot describe it. Those piercing eyes seemed to read one's very soul; power and authority sat on that ample brow; while the deep lines on the forehead and face implied an age which the jet-black hair and beard flowing down in indistinguishable luxuriance almost to the waist seemed to belie. No need to ask in whose presence I stood, as I bowed myself before one who is the object of a devotion and love which kings might envy and emperors sigh for in vain!

A mild dignified voice bade me be seated, and then continued: – 'Praise be to God that thou hast attained! . . . Thou hast come to see a prisoner and an exile . . . We desire but the good of the world and the happiness of the nations; yet they deem us a stirrer up of strife and sedition worthy of bondage and banishment . . . That all nations should become one in faith and all men as brothers; that the bonds of affection and unity between the sons of men should be strengthened; that diversity of religion should cease and differences of race be annulled – what harm is there in this? . . .

Yet so it shall be; these fruitless strifes, these ruinous wars shall pass away, and the "Most Great Peace" shall come . . . Do not you in Europe need this also? Is not this that which Christ foretold? . . . Yet do we see your kings and rulers lavishing their treasures more freely on means for the destruction of the human race than on that which would conduce to the happiness of mankind . . . These strifes and this bloodshed and discord must cease, and all men be as one kindred and one family . . . Let not a man glory in this, that he loves his country; let him rather glory in this, that he loves his kind . . .'

Such, so far as I can recall them, were the words which, besides many others, I heard from Behá. Let those who read them consider well with themselves whether such doctrines merit death and bonds, and whether the world is more likely to gain or lose by their diffusion.

Introduction to 'Abdu'l-Bahá, *Traveller's Narrative*, vol. 2, pp. xxxix–xi

◆

Bahá'u'lláh passed away on 29 May 1892 in the mansion of Bahjí and was buried in a nearby house. He was seventy-four years of age and had spent forty of those years as a prisoner and exile. In 1844, at the age of twenty-seven he had voluntarily given up the life of comfort and prestige that was his inheritance and entered the ranks of the poor and oppressed in the world. Like many millions in our world today, Bahá'u'lláh knew what it was like to lose home and possessions, to be stripped of all human rights, to be a prisoner and a refugee, to be subjected to unjust legal procedures and to be the victim of corrupt officials; in Tehran in 1852, he had experienced the anger of a mob whipped into blind and senseless rage; on the road to Baghdad, he and his family had suffered from poverty, hunger and exposure; during the course of his exiles, he and his wife had watched their children become ill and die; and in the early years in Akka, he had experienced overcrowded accommodation, lack of food, unhygienic conditions and the resultant diseases. When therefore Bahá'u'lláh writes of the need for society to look after the poor and disadvantaged and to guard against injustice and corruption, he is writing of things he had experienced at first hand and about which he cared deeply. His shrine is regarded by Bahá'ís as the holiest place on earth.

'ABDU'L-BAHÁ

Bahá'u'lláh appointed his eldest son, 'Abdu'l-Bahá (translated as 'the servant of Bahá'), as the leader of the Bahá'í community (the Centre of the Covenant as this is called in the Bahá'í writings) and the sole authorized interpreter of his writings. 'Abdu'l-Bahá, whose given name was 'Abbás, was born in Tehran on 23 May 1844, the day that saw the start of the Báb's mission.

From the earliest years of his ministry, 'Abdu'l-Bahá was opposed by his half-brother, Mírzá Muhammad 'Alí. The latter claimed that 'Abdu'l-Bahá was exceeding his authority. At first, Mírzá Muhammad 'Alí succeeded in obtaining the support of several influential Bahá'ís. In the end, however, his opposition faded away and the overwhelming majority of Bahá'ís supported 'Abdu'l-Bahá. This was undoubtedly mainly due to the clear and unequivocal text of Bahá'u'lláh's Book of My Covenant in which 'Abdu'l-Bahá's appointment was made.

The main result of the opposition of 'Abdu'l-Bahá's half-brother was the reimposition of the strict terms of the original government orders of exile. This confined 'Abdu'l-Bahá to the city of Akka for some five years. Eventually, as a result of the Young Turks Revolution in 1908, 'Abdu'l-Bahá was freed. One of his first actions was to complete the shrine of the Báb on Mount Carmel and to place the remains of the Báb there.

During the early years of 'Abdu'l-Bahá's ministry, the Bahá'í Faith was taken to North America. By the turn of the twentieth century, there was a community of several thousand Bahá'ís in North America. Some small groups also arose in Europe. This was a very significant turning point in the development of the Bahá'í Faith. It demonstrated that the Bahá'í Faith was capable of appealing to people outside the cultural world of the Middle East, to which it had been confined up to that time. After he was freed in 1908, 'Abdu'l-Bahá moved to Egypt for a while before setting off on the first of two journeys to the West. On the first journey, in 1911, 'Abdu'l-Bahá visited France and England. Then in 1912–13, he visited North America, Great Britain, France, Germany and Hungary. In all these places he spoke at public meetings, in churches and before a wide variety of associations. He spoke on many of the issues of that time: peace, women's rights, racial equality, labour relations, etc. He met many prominent politicians, philosophers, artists, scientists and leaders of thought, and attracted a great deal of attention from newspapers and magazines.

'Abdu'l-Bahá returned to Haifa in 1913 and the following year the First World War broke out, cutting off communications with the outside world. During these war years, 'Abdu'l-Bahá wrote the Tablets of the Divine Plan, laying down his instructions for the worldwide spread of the Bahá'í Faith.

At the end of the war, the Haifa–Akka area fell to the British army and Palestine came under the British mandate. 'Abdu'l-Bahá was much respected by the British authorities, and he was eventually knighted for his services. 'Abdu'l-Bahá passed away on 28 November 1921 and is buried in one of the rooms of the shrine of the Báb.

SHOGHI EFFENDI

In his Will and Testament, 'Abdu'l-Bahá appointed his eldest grandson, Shoghi Effendi, as leader of the Bahá'í community (the Guardian of the Bahá'í Faith) and as the authorized interpreter of the Bahá'í scriptures.

During the early years of Shoghi Effendi's ministry there were several episodes of persecution of Bahá'í communities. In Iran in 1926–7, there were several outbursts in which Bahá'ís were killed, and again in 1934, wide-ranging official measures were taken against the Bahá'ís. From 1926 onwards, the Soviet authorities increasingly persecuted the Bahá'í communities in the Caucasus and Central Asia. In 1928, they expropriated the Mashriqu'l-Adhkár (see pp. 74–5) that the Bahá'ís had built in Ashkhabad. In 1922, the house that Bahá'u'lláh had occupied in Baghdad, a site of pilgrimage for Bahá'ís, was taken over. Despite winning their case before the League of Nations in 1928, the Bahá'ís were never able to regain possession of it.

Shoghi Effendi spent the first fifteen years of his ministry establishing and assuring the proper functioning of the Bahá'í administrative structure. He then began to use this administration in a series of plans to extend the geographical range of the Bahá'í Faith. In 1937, he gave the American Bahá'ís the task of taking the Bahá'í Faith to several countries in Central and South America. Over the next few years he gave plans to various national Bahá'í communities. He gave the Iranian and Egyptian Bahá'ís the task of spreading the Bahá'í Faith to the Arab countries, the Indian Bahá'ís to South-East Asia; the British Bahá'ís to Africa; and he gave the American Bahá'ís a further plan involving Latin America and Europe. The culmination of all this was a Ten-Year World Crusade (1953–63) which was to open many of the remaining countries of the world to the Bahá'í Faith.

During the Ten-Year Crusade, a development occurred that was eventually to change the face of the Bahá'í Faith. In widely separate corners of the world such as Uganda, Bolivia, Indonesia and India, large numbers of poor, illiterate villagers and tribal peoples began to join the Bahá'í community.

Shoghi Effendi passed away in 1957 during a stay in London, where he is buried. The Bahá'í world continued to be administered until the end of the Ten-Year World Crusade in 1963 by a group of individuals whom Shoghi Effendi had designated 'Hands of the Cause of God' and whom he had called the 'chief stewards of Bahá'u'lláh's embryonic World Commonwealth'. In 1963, the Universal House of Justice (see pp. 70–1 and below), a body envisaged in Bahá'u'lláh's writings, was established by election.

THE UNIVERSAL HOUSE OF JUSTICE

Since its establishment in 1963, the Universal House of Justice has been the highest authority in the Bahá'í world. It directs the affairs of the Bahá'í Faith at the international level and provides guidance and co-ordination for the activities of the various National Spiritual Assemblies.

The Universal House of Justice has launched successive plans for the spread and consolidation of Bahá'í communities around the world. These plans have been: the Nine-Year Plan (1964–73); the Five-Year Plan (1973–9); the Seven-Year Plan (1979–86); the Six-Year Plan (1986–92); the Three-Year Plan (1993–6); and the Four-Year Plan (1996–2000). In broad outline these plans have included the tasks of:

● spreading the Bahá'í Faith to all parts of the globe and increasing the number of its adherents

- establishing and improving the functioning of the Bahá'í administrative order in all parts of the world and accelerating the maturation of the national and local Bahá'í communities so that they take on more of the functions envisaged for them in the Bahá'í teachings
- encouraging the individual spiritual development of all Bahá'ís as well as their universal participation in all aspects of Bahá'í community life
- improving the qualitative aspects of Bahá'í community and family life, especially through a wider extension of Bahá'í education
- promoting the greater involvement of Bahá'ís in the life of human society, and in particular the pursuit of projects of social and economic development in well-established Bahá'í communities
- increasing worldwide the translation, production, distribution and use of Bahá'í literature
- proclaiming the message of Bahá'u'lláh to all strata of society and minority groups
- developing the Bahá'í World Centre as the spiritual and administrative focus of the world Bahá'í community
- collecting, classifying and making available the writings of the central figures of the Bahá'í Faith
- erecting, as resources allow, further Bahá'í Houses of Worship, the Mashriqu'l-Adhkárs
- extending the relationships of the international Bahá'í community with international organizations such as the United Nations and its subsidiary organs

A notable feature of the most recent plans has been the increasing extent to which responsibility for drawing up and monitoring the plans has been devolved away from the Bahá'í World Centre towards the national and local Bahá'í communities.

9 THE BAHÁ'Í WORLD TODAY

The Bahá'í world today is a community that is extremely diverse in its ethnicity and in the social, cultural and religious background of its adherents. Despite its diversity, it is managing to work together to pursue goals of international co-operation and development. In view of this, the Universal House of Justice in a recent message called upon the people of the world to consider the Bahá'í world community as a model for the future unification of humanity.

THE EXPANSION OF THE BAHÁ'Í COMMUNITY

The expansion of the Bahá'í Faith takes place mainly through the person-to-person contact of individual Bahá'ís with their neighbours and friends. Those who express an interest are invited to a 'fireside', an informal gathering usually held in the home of one of the Bahá'ís. In some countries, however, especially in the villages of the poorer countries of the world, the Bahá'í Faith has been proclaimed and accepted by large numbers of people at one time.

There is no ritual or ceremony of conversion. If someone accepts the claims that Bahá'u'lláh has made about his station and mission, agrees to follow the Bahá'í laws, and accepts the station of Bahá'u'lláh's successors, 'Abdu'l-Bahá and Shoghi Effendi, as well as the authority of the Universal House of Justice, which was ordained by Bahá'u'lláh, then that person is a Bahá'í. In order to become part of the worldwide Bahá'í community, however, it is usually necessary to register with one's local Bahá'í community.

The spread of the Bahá'í Faith from one country to another usually occurs through the movement of individual Bahá'ís called 'pioneers'. There are no professional missionaries, and Bahá'í pioneers will usually take up employment or start a business in their new locations. The spread of the Bahá'í Faith around the world has been organized through a series of systematic plans begun under Shoghi Effendi and continued by the Universal House of Justice (see pp. 127–9).

Currently there are Bahá'í communities in every country in the world except the Vatican. This makes the Bahá'í Faith the second most widely spread religion in the world, after Christianity; a statement that is supported by authoritative publications such as the *Britannica Book of the Year*[1] and the *World Christian Encyclopedia*.[2] Organized Bahá'í communities exist in most countries, except where persecution and official prohibition of the Bahá'í Faith make this impossible.

As a whole, the Bahá'í Faith has been rapidly increasing in numbers. In the early 1950s, there were probably some 200,000 Bahá'ís in the world. This had increased to about a million by the late 1960s, about four and a half million by the late 1980s, and over five million by the mid-1990s. Something of the impact of this tremendous rate of growth in recent years can be gleaned from the fact that as recently as the early 1950s, over 90 per cent of all the Bahá'ís of the world were Iranians. Now Iranians constitute only about 6 per cent of the world Bahá'í population.

The number of National and Local Spiritual Assemblies has also increased in proportion to the rise in numbers of Bahá'ís. This increase can best be seen in the table on the following page.

The largest Bahá'í communities are in the countries of the Third World: South America, sub-Saharan Africa, the Pacific, and South and South-East Asia. The largest Bahá'í community in the world is in India, where they number some two million. The size of the population of India, however, means that the Bahá'ís are still only a very small proportion of the population. It is in the countries of the Pacific that the Bahá'ís form the largest proportion of the population. In countries such as Kiribati and the Marshall Islands, the Bahá'ís form 12–18 per cent of the total population.

Such a rapid increase in numbers has produced its own problems, and growth in some areas paused for a time while attempts were made to

GROWTH IN THE INSTITUTIONS OF THE BAHÁ'Í FAITH

	1954	1963	1968	1973	1979	1988	1994
National Spiritual Assemblies	12	56	81	113	125	149	172
Local Spiritual Assemblies	708	3,379	5,902	17,037	23,634	19,486	17,780
Localities where Bahá'ís reside	3,117	11,092	31,883	69,541	102,704	112,137	119,276

NOTES: Figures taken from P. Smith and M. Momen, *The Baha'i Faith 1957–1988*, p. 70 and *The Bahá'í World, 1994–5*, p. 317. The drop in the number of Local Spiritual Assemblies between 1979 and 1988 is accounted for by a major reorganization in 1987 in India where the area for each Local Spiritual Assembly was increased to cover more than one village. The result was a drop in the number of Local Spiritual Assemblies in India from 15,448 to 4,497. There have since been similar reorganizations in other countries.

deepen the knowledge and experience of the new Bahá'ís. The introduction of social and economic development projects has broadened the range of activities in many of these Bahá'í communities.

Although the Bahá'í Faith began in the Middle East, continued persecution in this region has severely limited its growth there. The Bahá'í Faith is banned in many Islamic countries and there have been sporadic persecutions in some of these countries such as Morocco, Egypt, Iraq, Iran and Indonesia. The most notable case of persecution has been in the Islamic Republic of Iran, where the Bahá'ís are the largest non-Muslim religious minority. Since the revolution of 1979, the Bahá'ís in Iran have been subjected to a relentless programme of persecution which has seen the leading Bahá'ís executed or driven into exile and the remaining Bahá'ís systematically looted of their property and stripped of all rights. Some Muslim countries have, however, exhibited tolerance. In Pakistan, for example, the Bahá'í Faith is officially recognized as a non-Muslim minority.

Bahá'ís have been present in the countries of the West (Europe, North America, Australia and New Zealand) since the time of 'Abdu'l-Bahá. Bahá'í communities in continental Europe were severely disrupted by the Second World War (during which there was Nazi persecution of the German Bahá'í community) and its aftermath (several existing Bahá'í communities fell into the communist bloc and Bahá'í activities ceased in these countries). Although the German Bahá'í community made a slow recovery after the war, the Bahá'í communities in the communist bloc did not re-emerge until the fall of communism at the end of the 1980s. There was then a rapid growth of the Bahá'í Faith in Eastern Europe such that the largest Bahá'í communities in Europe now include such countries as Romania and Albania. In North America, Western Europe, Australia and New Zealand, there has been slow but steady growth.

The Bahá'í communities in South and Central America have their origins in the activities of the North American Bahá'ís in the late 1930s and the 1940s. From the mid-1950s onwards there was a sudden dramatic increase in the number of Bahá'ís in this region. This was the result of a large number of conversions among native Amerindians, in such countries as Bolivia, Ecuador and Panama.

The Bahá'í Faith did not really establish itself in any systematic way in sub-Saharan Africa until the 1950s, when Bahá'ís settled in many newly emerging independent nations. There was then rapid growth in a few countries such as Uganda, and a gradual expansion into other countries. Outbreaks of persecution or civil unrest have hampered the development of the Bahá'í Faith in many African countries. In those countries where this has not occurred, the Bahá'í community has grown considerably.

The Bahá'í Faith has had a presence in South Asia since the time of Bahá'u'lláh. Until the 1960s, however, almost all the Indian Bahá'ís were from either Muslim or Zoroastrian backgrounds. Since that time, however, increasing numbers of villagers of Hindu background have been enrolled. There are also substantial Bahá'í communities in Pakistan and Bangladesh.

In South-East Asia, there was a rapid spread of the Bahá'í Faith in the 1950s and 1960s, especially in Indonesia, Malaysia, Vietnam and the Philippines. After this time, there was a divergence in the fortunes of these Bahá'í communities. In some countries, such as Indonesia and Vietnam, the Bahá'ís were subjected to persecution, while in other countries expansion continued.

In East Asia, expansion has been slow. The Bahá'í Faith is not recognized in the People's Republic of China or in North Korea, so there is no organized Bahá'í activity in those countries. Even in countries such as Japan and South Korea where there is religious freedom, however, the position of the Bahá'í Faith resembles that of Western Europe, with only a slow rate of increase.

Although Bahá'í communities had existed in Central Asia up to the time of the First World War, these were persecuted and decimated after the communist takeover. Since the collapse of communism, there has been a steady growth of Bahá'í communities in all the nations of this region.

Apart from Hawaii, where there has been a Bahá'í community since the time of 'Abdu'l-Bahá, there were only isolated Bahá'ís in other parts of the Pacific until the 1950s. Since the 1960s there has been significant growth in most of the island groups. The Bahá'ís now form a substantial minority of the population in many of the island nations of the Pacific.

CO-OPERATION WITH THE UNITED NATIONS AND OTHER INTERNATIONAL AGENCIES

The Bahá'í community has had a close relationship with the United Nations ever since its formation. Bahá'ís do not consider the present structure and constitution of the United Nations to be the best possible. They nevertheless consider its ideals to be close to those of the Bahá'í Faith and therefore worthy of full support.

Over the last few decades, the Bahá'í International Community has been one of the most active of the non-governmental organizations at the United Nations. It has had consultative status with many of the subsidiary organizations of the United Nations (such as ECOSOC, UNICEF, etc.) and also a significant presence at all of the major United Nations conferences. It has presented position papers and seminars at most of them. In addition, the Bahá'í community has supported the various campaigns and special years that the United Nations has launched. With the establishment of an Office of the Environment (in

1989), and an Office for the Advancement of Women (in 1992), the Bahá'í International Community has been able to devote greater attention to these areas of concern.

SOCIAL AND ECONOMIC DEVELOPMENT PROJECTS

Although several attempts were made as early as the closing decades of the nineteenth century in the Iranian Bahá'í community to begin projects for social development, these did not flourish because of the repression of the Bahá'í community. The numerous schools started by the Iranian Bahá'ís, for example, were all closed in 1934 on the orders of the government.

Recent decades have seen the emergence of large Bahá'í communities in the poorer parts of the world, which has led to a renewed impetus towards social and economic development plans. These plans (as described on pp. 63–6) are usually developed by the local communities with some assistance from the national level.

In each area of the world, the nature of the development projects has varied according to the needs of the area and the possibilities open to the Bahá'ís. In South America, there are many Bahá'ís among the native Amerindian tribes of the Andes. The difficulty of travelling over the mountainous terrain has led to the development of several Bahá'í radio stations. These can broadcast programmes on health, agriculture and literacy as well as programmes about the Bahá'í Faith to the people in their own languages. One of the major problems faced by the native peoples in this area is the downgrading of the Amerindian culture in favour of the Hispanic European culture. The Bahá'í radio stations have played a major role in the revival of native American culture through native music and the retelling of stories.

In India, the Bahá'ís have adopted a different approach. A number of institutions have been created to which key people from villages can be brought. There they are taught skills and knowledge which they then take back to their villages and teach to others. The skills taught at these institutes include literacy, rural technology, health and hygiene, and crafts for women to enable them to earn a living. The participants are also taught about the Bahá'í teachings and the functioning of Bahá'í communities. Similar institutes have been used in a number of other places such as Kivu province in Zaire and among the Guaymi Indians in Panama.

Because of the emphasis on education in Bahá'í teachings, many Bahá'í projects have focused on schools. One model is that of the tutorial school, where one or two teachers, who have been specially trained for this work, conduct classes for children and adults, often in the open air. Subjects taught include reading, writing, character training and other relevant subjects. This pattern has been successful in countries as diverse as India, Zaire, Bolivia and the Philippines. As of 1992, there were 116 Bahá'í academic schools, 62 kindergartens and 488 tutorial schools throughout the Bahá'í world. The vast majority of these were in developing countries, serving largely rural areas or small towns.

In view of the Bahá'í teaching that it is necessary to advance the social role of women, many Bahá'í projects are oriented towards women. In India, for example, the Bahá'í Vocational Institute for Rural Women at Indore offers village women residential courses on literacy, health care and income-generating skills. Its success has been widely recognized and it won one of the Global 500 Environmental Action Awards that were awarded at the Earth Summit in Rio de Janiero in 1992.

All Bahá'í projects are open to all the inhabitants of the area in which they take place, both to participate in and to benefit from. Neither the schools nor other projects are ever restricted to Bahá'ís or any other special segment of the populace. This is in keeping with the Bahá'í ethos of the oneness of humanity.

Bahá'í youth have contributed in an important way to many projects around the world. Giving up a year or more to the service of the Bahá'í Faith and to humanity as a whole has increasingly become a standard part of the lives of Bahá'í youth when they finish school or university.

THE BAHÁ'Í COMMUNITY AS A MODEL

The present period is one in which humanity is in an ideological crisis. By the beginning of the twentieth century, religion had ceased, at least in Europe, to play a central role in determining the vision and values of society. During the course of the twentieth century, humanity has experimented with a number of ideologies in an attempt to fill the vacuum left by religion at the centre of society. Nationalism, racism and communism have all been tried and have all spectacularly failed, leaving behind destruction on a massive scale. The strident nationalism of the European states brought about the First World War and the consequent ruin of large parts of Europe. Racist ideologies led to the Nazi concentration camps and the destruction of the Second World War. Although Europe was the first to be affected, other parts of the world have had similar experiences. More recently, we have seen communism falter and fail, leaving behind a legacy of shattered economies and environmental devastation.

There are two major contenders competing to fill the ideological vacuum that now exists. One is free-market capitalism, which, at the present time, is principally a combination of *laissez-faire* economics and strident individualism and consumerism. The dominant place of this ideology in society is a paradox in that this ideology is itself destructive of society. For the adherents of this philosophy, government and regulation are evils, and should be reduced to a minimum in order to allow the forces of the market to have a free run. There can be little doubt that the pursuit of free-market capitalism by a number of countries, and the individualism and consumerism that are inherent aspects of it, have resulted in a widening of the gap between the rich and poor in those countries, with a consequent deterioration of urban life. The Universal House of Justice has commented on the tendency of this ideology to

> callously abandon starving millions to the operations of a market system that all too clearly is aggravating the plight of the majority of mankind, while enabling small sections to live in a condition of affluence scarcely dreamed of by our forebears . . . The time has come when those who preach the dogmas of . . . capitalism . . . must give account of the moral stewardship they have presumed to exercise. Where is the 'new world' promised by these ideologies? Where is the international peace to whose ideals they proclaim their devotion? Where are the breakthroughs into new realms of cultural achievement . . .? Why is the vast majority of the world's peoples sinking ever deeper into hunger and wretchedness when wealth on a scale undreamed of by the Pharaohs, the Caesars, or even the imperialist powers of the nineteenth century is at the disposal of the present arbiters of human affairs?[3]

The other major contender to fill the ideological vacuum at the centre of world society is religious fundamentalism. The basic premise of this movement is as follows: if the ideological experiments of the twentieth century have failed, then let us return to the previous situation when traditional religion was the central ideology of society. In almost every major religion, there exists a fundamentalist movement seeking to bring about a return to a perceived golden past of morality and social responsibility. Unfortunately for the fundamentalists, a basic element of that past situation was that the religious viewpoint was not only the dominant viewpoint of society, it was the only viewpoint. The arts, literature, science, medicine, charitable works, all aspects of social life were dominated and controlled by religion, and no competitor existed. From the time of the Renaissance, and particularly with the coming of the Enlightenment, alternative ideologies emerged which competed successfully with religion. With the passing of time, it became possible to see the world in other ways, from the perspective of scientific rationalism, for example. One by one, science, the arts, literature, medicine and even charitable works escaped the control of religion because alternative frameworks were found to be better, and it is almost impossible now for religious fundamentalists to return society to the previous situation, where no alternative was even conceived.

It is the belief of Bahá'ís, that these two alternatives, capitalism and religious fundamentalism, which appear at present to be the only viable ideologies on the world scene, are likely to fail as have the other ideologies of the twentieth century, such as nationalism, racism and communism. Each of these ideologies continues to have its proponents and supporters but it is not possible to see, at present, what they can offer humanity other than disunity and disintegration. As Shoghi Effendi commented:

> If long-cherished ideals and time-honoured institutions, if certain social assumptions and religious formulae have ceased to promote the welfare of the generality of mankind, if they no longer minister to the needs of a continually evolving humanity, let them be swept away and relegated to the limbo of obsolescent and forgotten doctrines. Why should these, in a world subject to the immutable law of change and decay, be exempt from the deterioration that must needs overtake every human institution? For legal standards, political and economic theories are solely designed to

safeguard the interests of humanity as a whole, and not humanity to be crucified for the preservation of the integrity of any particular law or doctrine.[4]

Bahá'ís would maintain that their religion presents a viable alternative to the choices that humanity is facing at present. On the one hand it presents a unified and integrated vision of the direction in which humanity should be proceeding. In a similar manner to the way that religion acted in the past, it presents an overall view of the world that colours everything; its teachings have some relevance to almost every aspect of the individual's personal life and human society as a whole. This does not mean, however, that it has the same aim as religious fundamentalists. The key difference between the Bahá'í Faith and the main established religions of the world is the fact that its vision was created within the last hundred years, and so has an immediacy and relevance that visions that had their origins a thousand years ago or more lack. Thus, for example, several of the established religions have been discredited in the eyes of many people or have split into deep divisions over such issues as scientific theories (for example, the debate over evolution) or the position of women in society. The Bahá'í view on such subjects, however, is compatible with a modern outlook and, because it is based on scripture, is not a cause of division within its ranks.

The Bahá'í Faith presents a unique integrated vision of the present state of the world and its future direction. This vision embraces politics, economics, environmental considerations, social issues, social administration, community development, ethical issues and spirituality. For Bahá'ís this vision is not just a utopian dream; Bahá'ís around the world are actively working for it.

Bahá'ís envisage the eventual creation of a world order which will bring about peace and reconciliation among the nations of the world. Bahá'ís believe, however, that this can only be achieved on the basis of the teachings that Bahá'u'lláh has given. The Bahá'í community worldwide is attempting to put into practice and give concrete shape to these teachings. It is taking positive steps towards peace and reconciliation between antagonistic groups and factions in society; it is helping to promote the role of women in society; it is promoting education, health and agriculture; it is making decisions and adopting policies by consultative means and without partisan politics and factional disputes; and it is building up social structures that are based on power being held by elected bodies and not by powerful individuals and cliques. In these ways, it may be considered a model for the kind of future that will give each individual the best opportunity for self-development and self-fulfilment. In its message addressed to the peoples of the world in 1985, the Universal House of Justice stated:

> The experience of the Bahá'í community may be seen as an example of this enlarging unity. It is a community of some three to four million people drawn from many nations, cultures, classes and creeds, engaged in a wide range of activities serving the spiritual, social and economic needs of the peoples of many lands. It is a single social organism, representative of the diversity of the human family, conducting its affairs through a system of commonly accepted consultative principles, and cherishing equally all the great outpourings of divine guidance in human history. Its existence is yet another convincing proof of the practicality of its Founder's vision of a united world, another evidence that humanity can live as one global society, equal to whatever challenges its coming of age may entail. If the Bahá'í experience can contribute in whatever measure to reinforcing hope in the unity of the human race, we are happy to offer it as a model for study.[5]

NOTES

1. THE INDIVIDUAL

1. *Tablets of Bahá'u'lláh*, p. 138.
2. Hidden Words, Arabic no. 56.
3. *Gleanings*, no. 153, pp. 328–9.
4. 'This present life is even as a swelling wave, or a mirage, or drifting shadows. Could ever a distorted image on the desert serve as refreshing waters? No, by the Lord of Lords!' (*Selections*, no. 150, pp. 177–8).
5. *Selections*, no. 188, pp. 220–1.
6. *Selections*, no. 170, p. 200.
7. 'Ages have passed and your precious lives are well-nigh ended, yet not a single breath of purity hath reached Our court of holiness from you' (Bahá'u'lláh, Hidden Words, Persian no. 20).
8. Hidden Words, Persian no. 40.
9. *Seven Valleys*, p. 5.
10. *Seven Valleys*, pp. 5, 7.
11. *Seven Valleys*, p. 7.
12. *Gleanings*, no. 128, pp. 274–5.
13. *Gleanings*, no. 71, p. 137.
14. Hidden Words, Persian no. 14.
15. *Gleanings*, no. 9, p. 12.
16. Hidden Words, Persian no. 45.
17. *Seven Valleys*, pp. 10–11.
18. *Seven Valleys*, p. 11.
19. *Seven Valleys*, pp. 11–13.
20. *Gleanings*, no. 27, p. 65.
21. *Promulgation of Universal Peace*, p. 4.
22. *Some Answered Questions*, pp. 235–6.
23. *Gleanings*, no. 100, p. 203.
24. *Tablets of Bahá'u'lláh*, p. 157.
25. Hidden Words, Arabic no. 2.
26. *Tablets of Bahá'u'lláh*, p. 64.
27. *Tablets of Bahá'u'lláh*, p. 38.
28. *Paris Talks*, p. 160.
29. *Paris Talks*, pp. 35–7.
30. *Paris Talks*, pp. 36–7.
31. *Epistle to the Son of the Wolf*, p. 15.
32. *Selections*, no. 1, pp. 1–2
33. *Selections*, no. 194, p. 233.
34. *Tablets of Bahá'u'lláh*, p. 37.
35. *Tablets of Bahá'u'lláh*, p. 37.
36. *Epistle to the Son of the Wolf*, p. 138.
37. Bahá'u'lláh quoted in Shoghi Effendi, *Advent of Divine Justice*, p. 26.
38. *Gleanings*, no. 136, p. 297.
39. *Gleanings* no. 91, p. 181.
40. *Advent of Divine Justice*, p. 3.
41. Hidden Words, Persian no. 44.
42. *Lights of Guidance*, no. 1156, p. 344.
43. *Gleanings*, no. 60, p. 118.
44. Hidden Words, Persian no. 5.
45. *Tablets of Bahá'u'lláh*, p. 156.
46. Hidden Words, Persian no. 76.
47. *Gleanings*, no. 128, p. 276.
48. *Gleanings*, no. 117, p. 250.
49. *Kitáb-i-Aqdas*, v. 33, p. 30; cf. *Tablets of Bahá'u'lláh*, p. 26.
50. *Seven Valleys*, p. 51.
51. *Paris Talks*, p. 110.
52. *Selections*, no. 137, p. 157.

53. *Selections*, no. 133, pp. 151–2.
54. *Promulgation of Universal Peace*, pp. 170–1.

2. THE FAMILY

1. *Selections*, no. 86, p. 118.
2. *Selections*, no. 84, pp. 117–18.
3. *Lights of Guidance*, no. 1268, pp. 378–9.
4. *Selections*, no. 92, p. 122.
5. *Selections*, no. 86, p. 118.
6. Bahá'u'lláh, *Kitáb-i-Aqdas*, v. 70, p. 44.
7. Written on behalf of Shoghi Effendi, *Compilation of Compilations*, vol. 1, no. 539, p. 241.
8. *Compilation of Compilations*, vol.1, no. 839, p. 391.
9. 'Abdu'l-Bahá, *Selections*, no. 113, p. 138.
10. Letter of Universal House of Justice in *Compilation of Compilations*, vol. 1, p. 414.
11. *Selections*, no. 836, p. 279.
12. Shoghi Effendi in *Compilation of Compilations*, vol. 1, no. 916, p. 413.
13. 'Abdu'l-Bahá, *Promulgation of Universal Peace*, p. 168
14. *Bahá'í World Faith*, pp. 329–30.
15. 'Abdu'l-Bahá in *Compilation of Compilations*, vol. 1, no. 590, p. 263.
16. Abdu'l-Bahá, *Selections*, no. 114, p. 139.
17. *Tablets of Bahá'u'lláh*, p. 162.
18. *Selections*, no. 103, pp. 129–31.
19. *Selections*, no. 103, p. 130.
20. *Bahá'í World Faith*, p. 399.
21. *Compilation of Compilations*, vol. 1, no. 603, p. 268; no. 622, p. 278; no. 628–9, pp. 282–3.
22. *Selections*, no. 95, pp. 124–5.
23. *Some Answered Questions*, pp. 8–9.
24. *Compilation of Compilations*, vol. 1, nos. 630–1, 635, pp. 284, 286.
25. *Epistle to the Son of the Wolf*, pp. 26–7.

3. SOCIETY

1. Hidden Words, Arabic no. 68.
2. *Promulgation of Universal Peace*, p. 316.
3. *Promulgation of Universal Peace*, p. 316.
4. *Promulgation of Universal Peace*, p. 316.
5. *Compilation of Compilations*, vol. 2, no. 2093, p. 357.
6. *Promulgation of Universal Peace*, pp. 135–7.
7. *Compilation of Compilations*, vol. 2, no. 2178, p. 391.
8. *Paris Talks*, p. 161.
9. *Selections*, no. 227, p. 302.
10. *Paris Talks*, p. 133.
11. Quoted in Esslemont, *Bahá'u'lláh and the New Era*, p. 141; or *Compilation of Compilations*, vol. 2, no. 2116, p. 369.
12. *Selections*, no. 38, pp. 79–80.
13. *Paris Talks*, p. 143.
14. *Gleanings*, no. 164, pp. 342–3.
15. *Epistle to the Son of the Wolf*, p. 44.
16. *Selections*, no. 19, pp. 41–2.
17. Letter written on behalf of Shoghi Effendi, 17 February 1933, in *Conservation of the Earth's Resources*, p. 15.
18. *Gleanings*, no. 159, pp. 335–6.
19. *Tablets of Bahá'u'lláh*, p. 169.
20. *Promulgation of Universal Peace*, pp. 230–1.
21. *Promulgation of Universal Peace*, p. 182.
22. *Promulgation of Universal Peace*, p. 217.
23. *Foundations of World Unity*, p. 39.
24. *Tablets of Bahá'u'lláh*, pp. 89–90.
25. *Foundations of World Unity*, pp. 39–41.
26. *Tablets of Bahá'u'lláh*, p. 28.
27. *Gleanings*, no. 118, pp. 250–2; no. 116, pp. 247–9.
28. *Gleanings*, no. 118, pp. 250–2; no. 116, pp. 247–9.
29. *Gleanings*, no. 120, p. 254.
30. *Tablets of Bahá'u'lláh*, p. 127.
31. *Some Answered Questions*, pp. 268–70.
32. *Some Answered Questions*, pp. 268–71.
33. *Promulgation of Universal Peace*, pp. 238–9.
34. *Some Answered Questions*, pp. 273–7.

4. GLOBAL CONCERNS

1. *Gleanings*, no. 131, p. 286.

2. *Epistle to the Son of the Wolf,* p. 14.
3. *Tablets of Bahá'u'lláh,* p. 168.
4. Bahá'u'lláh, *Kitáb-i-Aqdas,* v. 58, p. 40; *Epistle to the Son of the Wolf,* p. 55; 'Abdu'l-Bahá, *Selections,* no. 225, p. 291.
5. *Gleanings,* no. 112, p. 218.
6. *Bahá'í World Faith,* pp. 257–8.
7. *Bahá'í World Faith,* pp. 258–9.
8. *Gleanings,* no. 117, pp. 249–50.
9. *Gleanings,* no. 43, p. 95.
10. *World Order of Bahá'u'lláh,* p. 41.
11. *World Order of Bahá'u'lláh,* p. 42.
12. *World Order of Bahá'u'lláh,* p. 42.
13. *World Order of Bahá'u'lláh,* pp. 42–3.
14. *Selections,* no. 15, p. 31.
15. *Selections,* no. 15, pp. 31–2.
16. *Gleanings,* no. 117, pp. 249–50.
17. *Gleanings,* no. 117, pp. 249–50.
18. *World Order of Bahá'u'lláh,* p. 203.
19. *World Order of Bahá'u'lláh,* p. 203.
20. *World Order of Bahá'u'lláh,* pp. 203–4.
21. *World Order of Bahá'u'llah,* p. 204.
22. *Gleanings,* no. 96, p. 213.
23. Bahá'u'lláh, *Tablets of Bahá'u'llah,* pp. 66–7.
24. *Compilation of Compilations,* no. 167, p. 93.

5. THE BAHÁ'Í COMMUNITY

1. *Will and Testament of 'Abdu'l-Bahá,* p. 14.
2. *Tablets of Bahá'u'lláh,* pp. 26–7.
3. *Costitution of the Universal House of Justice,* pp. 5–6.
4. *Promulgation of Universal Peace,* p. 65.
5. *Bahá'í Administration,* p. 63.
6. *Will and Testament of Abdu'l-Bahá,* p. 11.
7. *Tablets of the Divine Plan,* p. 49.
8. *Tablets of the Divine Plan,* p. 49.
9. *Compilation of Compilations,* vol. 1, no. 251, pp. 127.
10. *Compilation of Compilations,* vol. 1, no. 182, p. 97.
11. Cited in Shoghi Effendi, *Bahá'í Administration,* pp. 21–2.
12. *Compilation of Compilations,* vol. 1, no. 182, pp. 97–8.

13. *Advent of Divine Justice,* p. 35.
14. *Advent of Divine Justice,* pp. 35–6.

6. BAHÁ'Í LAWS

1. *Gleanings,* no. 43, p. 97.
2. *Kitáb-i-Aqdas,* v. 5, p. 21.
3. *Gleanings,* no. 155, p. 332.
4. *Kitáb-i-Aqdas,* v. 149, pp. 73–4.
5. *Bahá'í World Faith,* p. 368.
6. *Bahá'í World Faith,* p. 378.
7. *Directives from the Guardian,* pp. 27–8.
8. *Selections,* no. 35, p. 70.
9. *Bahá'í Prayers,* p . 105.
10. From a letter written on behalf of Shoghi Effendi, cited in *Lights of Guidance,* no. 1156, p. 344.
11. *Kitáb-i-Aqdas,* v. 65, p. 42.
12. *Kitáb-i-Aqdas,* v. 28, p. 28.
13. *Lights of Guidance,* no. 669, p. 201.
14. *Gleanings,* no. 125, p. 265.
15. *Kitáb-i-Aqdas,* v. 187, p. 87.
16. *Selections,* no. 138, p. 159.

7. THEOLOGICAL TEACHINGS

1. *Gleanings,* no. 26, p. 62.
2. *Gleanings,* no. 148, p. 316.
3. *Selections,* no. 31, p. 63.
4. *Selections,* no. 24, pp. 53–4.
5. *Gleanings,* no. 19, pp. 46–7.
6. *Gleanings,* no. 19, p. 47.
7. *Gleanings,* no. 19, p. 46.
8. *Gleanings,* no. 21, p. 50.
9. *Gleanings,* no. 22, p. 53.
10. *Gleanings,* no. 81, p. 157.
11. *Prayers and Meditations,* no. 58, p. 91. 'Abdu'l-Bahá asserts that allthings exist through God. *Some Answered Questions,* p. 293.
12. Hidden Words, Arabic no. 13.
13. *Gleanings,* no. 93, p. 189.
14. *Some Answered Questions,* pp. 9–10.
15. *Gleanings,* no. 34, pp. 79–80.
16. *Some Answered Questions,* pp. 147–8.
17. *Gleanings,* no. 155, p. 331.
18. *Gleanings,* no. 110, p. 215.
19. *Gleanings,* no. 43, p. 95.
20. *Will and Testament,* p. 14.
21. *Kitáb-i-Íqán,* p. 152.
22. *Kitáb-i-Íqán,* pp. 152–4.
23. *Kitáb-i-Íqán,* p. 176.
24. *Kitáb-i-Íqán,* p. 21.

25. *Gleanings*, no. 34, pp. 78–9.
26. *Kitáb-i-Íqán*, p. 177.
27. *Gleanings*, no. 34, p. 81.
28. Bahá'u'lláh, *Gleanings*, no. 109, p. 215.
29. *Gleanings*, no. 38, pp. 87–8.
30. Hidden Words, Arabic no. 67.
31. *Kitáb-i-Aqdas*, v. 1, p. 19.
32. Hidden Words, Arabic no. 40.
33. *Promulgation of Universal Peace*, p. 69.
34. *Seven Valleys*, pp. 21–2.
35. Hidden Words, Arabic no. 11.
36. Hidden Words, Persian no. 27.
37. *Gleanings*, no. 77, p. 149.
38. Hidden Words, Persian no. 26.
39. *Tablets of 'Abdu'l-Bahá*, vol. 2, p. 354.
40. *Seven Valleys*, pp. 17 –18.
41. *Seven Valleys*, p. 24.
42. *Seven Valleys*, p. 22.
43. Hidden Words, Persian no. 70.
44. *Seven Valleys*, pp. 31–2.
45. *Seven Valleys*, p. 36.
46. Hidden Words, Persian no. 29.
47. *Paris Talks*, pp. 178–9.
48. Hidden Words, Arabic no. 51.
49. *Bahá'í World Faith*, p. 372.

50. *Gleanings*, no. 82, pp. 158–9.
51. *Some Answered Questions*, p. 239.
52. *Some Answered Questions*, p. 228.
53. *Gleanings*, no. 81, p. 157.
54. *Promulgation of Universal Peace*, pp. 225–6.
55. *Promulgation of Universal Peace*, p. 226.
56. *Promulgation of Universal Peace*, p. 226.
57. *Promulgation of Universal Peace*, pp. 226–7.
58. *Gleanings*, no. 82, p. 161.
59. *Gleanings*, no. 82, pp. 161–2.
60. *Some Answered Questions*, p. 240.

8. THE HISTORY OF THE BAHÁ'Í FAITH

1. Quoted in Shoghi Effendi, *God Passes By*, pp. 101–2.

9. THE BAHÁ'Í WORLD TODAY

1. See article D. Barrett, 'Religion: World Religious Statistics'.
2. p. 6.
3. *Promise of World Peace*, pp. 6–7.
4. *World Order of Bahá'u'lláh*, p. 42.
5. *Promise of World Peace*, pp. 19–20.

BIBLIOGRAPHY

'Abdu'l-Bahá, *Foundations of World Unity*, comp. Horace Holley, Wilmette, IL: Bahá'í Publishing Trust, 1968.
— *Paris Talks: Addresses Given by 'Abdu'l-Bahá in Paris in 1911–1912*, 11th edn., London: Bahá'í Publishing Trust, 1979.
— *The Promulgation of Universal Peace*, comp. Howard MacNutt, 2nd edn., Wilmette, IL: Bahá'í Publishing Trust, 1982.
— *The Secret of Divine Civilization*, Wilmette, IL: Bahá'í Publishing Trust, 1990.
— *Selections from the Writings of 'Abdu'l-Bahá*, comp. Research Department of the Universal House of Justice and trans. by a committee at the Bahá'í World Centre and Marzieh Gail, Haifa: Bahá'í World Centre, 1978.
— *Some Answered Questions*, comp. and trans. Laura Clifford Barney, Wilmette, IL: Bahá'í Publishing Trust, 1981.
— *Tablets of 'Abdul Baha Abbas*, 3 vols., Chicago: Bahai Publishing Society, 1909–19.
— *Tablets of the Divine Plan*, rev. edn., Wilmette, IL: Bahá'í Publishing Trust, 1977.
— *A Traveller's Narrative Written to Illustrate the Episode of the Bab*, trans. Edward Granville Browne, 2 vols., Cambridge: Cambridge University Press, 1891.
— *Will and Testament of 'Abdu'l-Bahá*, Wilmette, IL: Bahá'í Publishing Committee, 1944.
Bahá'í Prayers, Wilmette, IL: Bahá'í Publishing Trust, 1985.
The Bahá'i World 1994–95, Haifa: Bahá'í World Centre, 1996.
Bahá'í World Faith, 2nd edn., Wilmette, IL: Bahá'í Publishing Trust, 1976.
Bahá'u'lláh, *Epistle to the Son of the Wolf*, trans. Shoghi Effendi, new edn., Wilmette, IL: Bahá'í Publishing Trust, 1988.
— *Gleanings from the Writings of Bahá'u'lláh*, comp. and trans. Shoghi Effendi, 2nd rev. edn., Wilmette, IL: Bahá'í Publishing Trust, 1976.
— *The Hidden Words of Bahá'u'lláh*, trans. by Shoghi Effendi with the assistance of some English friends, rev. edn., Wilmette, IL: Bahá'í Publishing Trust, 1979.
— *Kitáb-i-Aqdas, the Most Holy Book*, Haifa: Bahá'í World Centre, 1992.
— *The Kitáb-i-Íqán, the Book of Certitude*, trans. Shoghi Effendi, 2nd edn., Wilmette, IL: Bahá'í Publishing Trust, 1974.
— *Prayers and Meditations by Bahá'u'lláh*, trans. Shoghi Effendi, Wilmette, IL: Bahá'í Publishing Trust, 1979.
— *The Proclamation of Bahá'u'lláh to the Kings and Leaders of the World*. Haifa:

Bahá'í World Centre, 1972.
— The Seven Valleys and the Four Valleys, trans. Ali Kuli Khan and Marzieh Gail, 3rd rev. edn., Wilmette, IL: Bahá'í Publishing Trust, 1978.
— Tablets of Bahá'u'lláh Revealed After the Kitáb-i-Aqdas, comp. Research Department of the Universal House of Justice, trans. Habib Taherzadeh with assistance of a committee at the Bahá'í World Centre, Haifa: Bahá'í World Centre, 1978.
Blomfield, Lady (Sara Louisa), The Chosen Highway, Wilmette, IL: Bahá'í Publishing Trust, 1967.
Britannica Book of the Year for 1988, Chicago: Encyclopaedia Britannica, 1988.
The Compilation of Compilations: Prepared by the Universal House of Justice, 1963–1990, 2 vols., n.p. [Mona Vale, N.S.W.]: Bahá'í Publications Australia, 1991.
Conservation of the Earth's Resources, London: Bahá'í Publishing Trust, 1990.
Esslemont, John E., Bahá'u'lláh and the New Era, 4th edn., London: Bahá'í Publishing Trust, 1974.
Grundy, Julia M., Ten Days in the Light of `Akká, Wilmette, IL: Bahá'í Publishing Trust, 1979.
Ives, Howard Colby, Portals to Freedom, Oxford: George Ronald, 1983.
Lights of Guidance: A Bahá'í Reference File, comp. Helen Hornby, 2nd rev. & enl. edn., New Delhi: Bahá'í Publishing Trust, 1988.
Shoghi Effendi, The Advent of Divine Justice, Wilmette, IL: Bahá'í Publishing Trust, 1984.
— Bahá'í Administration, 1974 edn., Wilmette, IL: Bahá'í Publishing Trust, 1974.
— Directives from the Guardian, comp. Gertrude Garrida, New Delhi: Bahá'í Publishing Trust, 1973.
— God Passes By, Wilmette, IL: Bahá'í Publishing Trust, 1974.
— The World Order of Bahá'u'lláh: Selected Letters, 2nd rev. edn., Wilmette, IL: Bahá'í Publishing Trust, 1974.
Smith, P. and M. Momen, 'The Bahá'i Faith 1957–1988: a survey of contemporary developments', Religion 19 (1989), pp. 63–91.
Universal House of Justice, The Constitution of the Universal House of Justice, Haifa: Bahá'í World Centre, 1972.
— The Promise of World Peace, Haifa: Bahá'í World Centre, 1985.
World Christian Encyclopedia, ed. David B. Barrett, Nairobi: Oxford University Press, 1982.

FURTHER READING

In the following review, publication information is given only for those books not appearing in the bibliography.

Many general introductory books have been written about the Bahá'í Faith. Among the better known ones are: J. E. Esslemont, *Bahá'u'lláh and the New Era*; Peter Smith, *The Bahá'í Religion* (Oxford: George Ronald, 1988); John Huddleston, *The Earth Is But One Country* (3rd edn n.p. [London]: Bahá'í [Publishing Trust], 1988); William S. Hatcher and J. Douglas Martin, *The Bahá'í Faith: The Emerging Global Religion* (San Francisco: Harper & Row, 1984); and John Ferraby, *All Things Made New: A Comprehensive Outline of the Bahá'í Faith* (2nd rev. edn. London: Bahá'í Publishing Trust, 1987). One book specially written for young people is René Derkse, *What is the Bahá'í Faith?* (Oxford: George Ronald, 1987). A useful basic guide to Bahá'í terms and concepts is Wendi Momen, *A Basic Bahá'í Dictionary* (Oxford: George Ronald, 1989). An annual survey is published under the title *The Bahá'í World* (Haifa: Bahá'í World Centre).

The major translated works of Bahá'u'lláh include: the Kitáb-i-Aqdas (Most Holy Book), his book of laws; the Kitáb-i-Íqán (Book of Certitude), on the subject of religious history and the interpretation of scripture and prophecy; the Hidden Words, a book of spiritual and ethical aphorisms; and the Seven Valleys, a book about the mystical path. *Gleanings from the Writings of Bahá'u'lláh* and *Tablets of Bahá'u'lláh Revealed After the Kitáb-i-Aqdas* are two important compilations of the writings of Bahá'u'lláh.

'Abdu'l-Bahá wrote few books. The main works that we have from him are compilations of his letters and talks. These include *Some Answered Questions*, a book containing 'Abdu'l-Bahá's answers to a large number of questions on theological and philosophical themes; *Promulgation of Universal Peace* and *Paris Talks* on social issues; and *Selections from the Writings of 'Abdu'l-Bahá*. He also wrote *The Secret of Divine Civilization* (Wilmette, IL: Bahá'í

Publishing Trust, 1990), on the subject of the spiritual and moral foundations for social and economic development.

Shoghi Effendi's major works include *God Passes By*, a survey and interpretation of Bahá'í history. *Bahá'í Administration* and *The World Order of Bahá'u'lláh* are compilations of his letters on the subject of the Bahá'í administration; and *The Promised Day Is Come* (Wilmette, IL: Bahá'í Publishing Trust, 1980) contains his interpretation of modern history. There are also several compilations of his letters to various national Bahá'í communities.

Many compilations of the scriptures and authoritative texts of the Bahá'í Faith on various subjects have been published; see for example *Unto Him Shall We Return* (comp. Hushidar Motlagh, Wilmette, IL: Bahá'í Publishing Trust, 1985) on the human soul and life after death; *The Throne of the Inner Temple* (comp. Elias Zohoori, privately printed, Jamaica, 1985) on health; and *Waging Peace* (Los Angeles: Kalimát Press, 1985). A series of compilations has been issued by the Universal House of Justice. These have been published separately by the Bahá'í Publishing Trust, London, and compiled in *The Compilation of Compilations*.

The best brief general history of the Bahá'í Faith is Peter Smith, *A Short History of the Bahá'í Faith*, Oxford: Oneworld, 1995. Peter Smith has also written a lengthier academic work: *The Babi and Baha'i Religions: From Messianic Shi'ism to a World Religion* (Cambridge: Cambridge University Press, 1987). There are a number of histories dealing with specific periods of Bahá'í history. The best biography of Bahá'u'lláh is H. M. Balyuzi, *Bahá'u'lláh, the King of Glory* (Oxford: George Ronald, 1980). The same author has also written biographies of the Báb and 'Abdu'l-Bahá: *The Báb, the Herald of the Day of Days* (Oxford: George Ronald, 1973); and *'Abdu'l-Bahá, the Centre of the Covenant of Bahá'u'lláh* (2nd ed Oxford: George Ronald, 1987). Shoghi Effendi's widow has written a biography of him: Rúhíyyih Rabbani, *The Priceless Pearl* (London: Bahá'í Publishing Trust, 1969).

On spirituality, see J. A. MacLean, *Dimensions in Spirituality* (Oxford: George Ronald, 1995). On social and economic development, see Holly Hanson Vick, *Social and Economic Development: A Bahá'í Approach* (Oxford: George Ronald, 1989). On consultation, see John E. Kolstoe, *Consultation: A Universal Lamp of Guidance* (Oxford: George Ronald, 1985). On the Bahá'í holy places, see David S. Ruhe, *Door of Hope: A Century of the Bahá'í Faith in the Holy Land* (Rev. edn., Oxford: George Ronald, 1989). On the Mashriqu'l-Adhkár (House of Worship), see Julie Badiee, *An Earthly Paradise* (Oxford: George Ronald, 1992). On peace, see *Circle of Peace* (Los Angeles: Kalimát Press, 1986). On world government and global issues, see J. Tyson, *World Peace and World Government* (Oxford: George Ronald, 1986).

FURTHER INFORMATION

Further information about the Bahá'í Faith can be obtained from the National Spiritual Assembly of the Bahá'ís in each country. For the major English-speaking countries these are:

Australia: P.O. Box 285, Mona Vale, NSW 2103. Tel. 2–99132771

Canada: 7200 Leslie St., Thornhill, Toronto ON L3T 6L8.
Tel. 1–905–889–8168

New Zealand: P.O. Box 21 – 551, Henderson, Auckland 8.
Tel. 9–837–4866

United Kingdom: 27 Rutland Gate, London SW7 1PD.
Tel. 0171–584–2566

United States: 536 Sheridan Rd, Wilmette, IL 60091.
Tel. 1–800–228–64833 (or 1–847–869–9039)

Bahá'í can be found almost anywhere in the online world. Almost every major provider, such as Compuserve, Genie, Prodigy and America Online has its own Bahá'í forum, as does Fidonet. Some also have other Bahá'í activities, 'chat' times and Bahá'í archive materials. On the Internet, the World Wide Web has many Bahá'í home pages, which can be found by doing a search on the word 'Bahai'. A good starting place is the home page of the Bahá'í World Centre 'http://www.Bahai.org/' or of the Bahá'í Computer and Communications Association (BCCA): 'http://www.bcca.org/'. The text of almost all of the Bahá'í scriptures and other authoritative texts (including almost all of the references given in this book) as well as some introductory material can be downloaded by FTP at 'ftp.bwc.org'. Login with the user name 'ftp' and give your e-mail address for the password. This site may also be accessed on the World Wide Web at 'ftp://ftp.bwc.org/bahai'. There is a Bahá'í questions and discussion group on Usenet: 'soc.religion.bahai'. It is also possible to participate in this group in the form of an Internet mailing list by sending a message to: 'Bahai-Faith-Request@bcca.org'.

INDEX

'Abdu'l-Bahá ('Abbás), 126–7, 130, 132: in Akka, 20, 73, 126, 127; appointed leader of the Bahá'í Faith, 126; death of, 127; exile of, 3, 22, 126; imprisonment of, 3; teachings of, 23, 24, 25, 26, 29, 31, 33, 36–7, 39, 40, 44, 45, 47–8, 49, 52, 57, 58, 60, 67, 70, 89, 93, 96, 107, 109, 127; travels, 3, 126–7; writings of, 3, 6, 7, 13, 14, 15, 21, 23, 25–6, 26–7, 28, 30–1, 32, 35, 36, 38, 39, 40, 41, 44, 47–8, 52, 56, 60, 63, 75, 76–7, 78–80, 84–7, 88, 89, 90, 93, 96, 97, 106, 109–10, 111, 113, 114, 127

administrative structure and Bahá'í institutions, 3, 4, 39, 66, 67–75, 129: Auxiliary Boards, 71, 72; Continental Boards of Counsellors, 71, 72; elections, 81–2; Hands of the Cause, 71, 128; holy days, 74; International Conventions, 70; National Conventions, 68: see also Bahá'í World Centre; calendar; consultation; Local Spiritual Assemblies; Mashriqu'l-Adhkár;

National Spiritual Assemblies; Nineteen Day Feast; Regional Spiritual Assemblies; Universal House of Justice
agriculture, 45, 64, 140
Akka: Bahá'í World Centre, 3, 72; place of exile, 3; place of pilgrimage, 20, 73; shrines, 72, 118, 125, 126
Azal, Mírzá Yaḥyá, 121, 123

Báb, the (Sayyid 'Alí Muhammad Shírází), 3, 72, 115–18, 119, 120, 121, 126: death of, 118, 121; imprisonment of, 116–17; shrine of, 72, 118, 126; teachings of, 87, 116; travels, 115, 116; writings of, 85, 117, 120
Bábís, 115, 117–18, 119, 120, 121
Bahá'í World Centre, 3, 66, 69, 71, 72–3, 129: Centre for the Study of the Sacred Text, 72; International Bahá'í Archives, 72; International Bahá'í Library, 72; International Teaching Centre, 71, 72
Bahá'u'lláh (Mírzá Ḥusayn 'Alí

Núrí), 119–25, 126, 130: in
Akka, 3, 73, 123, 125; arrest of,
119; death of, 3, 125; 'Divine
Physician', 54, 76; exile of, 3, 22,
120, 121, 125; founder of Bahá'í
Faith, 3, 16, 20, 63, 73–4, 77, 78,
81, 83, 84, 102, 119, 120–1;
imprisonment of, 3, 119, 123,
125; letters to world leaders,
120–3; Manifestation of God,
101–2; shrine of, 72, 125;
teachings of, 7–9, 10, 12, 14,
15–17, 18–19, 20–1, 21–2, 23,
26, 27, 29, 34, 37, 40, 43–4,
45–6, 51, 52, 54–5, 58, 59, 61,
63, 65, 67, 76, 87, 88, 89, 90,
91–2, 94–5, 96, 97–101, 103,
105, 110, 120, 125, 139–40;
visionary experience, 119;
writings of, 3, 6–7, 8–9, 10, 11,
12, 13, 14, 15–16, 17–18, 18–19,
20–1, 24, 29, 30, 33, 35, 37–8,
40–1, 43–4, 46–7, 54–5, 56, 58,
60, 63, 65, 70, 77, 83, 84, 85, 87,
92, 93–4, 94–5, 96, 97–8, 99,
100–1, 102, 103, 104, 105,
106–7, 108, 110, 111, 112,
113–14, 119, 120, 123, 126
Bahjí, 72, 123, 125
Browne, Edward G., 124–5
Buddhism, 91, 92, 102, 103:
Buddha, 119, 121

calendar, 67, 73–4
chastity, 16–18, 24, 88
children, 27–9, 43
Christianity, 4, 102, 103, 105,
131
community relationships, 28, 34,
45, 47–8, 55, 64, 70
consultation, 28, 47, 64, 65, 66, 68,
78–80, 140
conversion, 103: to Bahá'í Faith,
103, 121, 128, 130, 133: see also
spread of Bahá'í Faith

death and burial, 70, 89–90
divorce, 26–7, 70, 89

economics, 2, 48–53, 62, 63–6, 70,
129
education, 25, 27, 29–33, 40, 43,
47–8, 51, 53, 64, 69, 95–6, 129,
140
environment, 40–2, 55, 62
equality, 2, 35, 36, 37–40, 53, 64,
81

family life, 25–34, 129: see also
children; education; marriage
fasting, 83, 86, 88
Five-Year Plan, 128
Four-Year Plan, 128
freedom, 21–2, 42–4, 55, 71
fundamentalism, religious, 138, 139

geographical distribution of Bahá'í
communities, 1, 3, 4: Africa, 1,
75, 128, 131, 133, 136; Arab
countries, 128; Australia, 75,
132, 133; Britain, 128; Caucasus,
124; Central America, 75, 128,
133, 136; Central Asia, 124, 134;
East Asia, 134; Egypt, 3, 124,
128; Europe, 3, 75, 126, 128,
132–3; India, 4, 75, 124, 128,
131, 135, 136; Iran, 3, 4, 128,
131; New Zealand, 132, 133;
North America, 3, 4, 68, 75, 126,
132, 133; Pacific, 1, 75, 131, 134;
Pakistan, 132; South America, 1,
128, 131, 133, 135; South Asia,
1, 4, 131, 133; South-East Asia,
128, 131, 133–4, 136
global perspective, 49, 50–1, 53,
54–66, 103, 139–40
God: beyond comprehension, 91–3,
94, 96; closeness to, 9, 84; and

equality, 37; humanity as reflection of, 104–5; love of, 49, 107, 113; Manifestations of, 93–7, 99–103; and marriage, 88; mercy of, 41; nature of, 91–5; search for, 8, 85, 86; and suffering, 108–10
government, 45–8, 61: relations with governments and other organizations, 70, 129, 134–5
Guardian of the Faith, see Shoghi Effendi

Haifa, see Akka
happiness and contentment, 5–7, 13, 16, 17, 21, 22, 23, 26, 29, 42, 48, 104, 106, 107
Hinduism, 91, 92, 102, 103, 133
history of the Bahá'í Faith, 3, 115–29
human rights, 43–5, 55, 71
humility, 8, 78
Ḥuqúqu'lláh, 65–6, 90

individualism, 42, 48, 51–2, 137
interconnectedness, 23, 41–2, 49
Islam, 102, 103, 115–16, 133

Jesus, 57, 98–9, 102, 119, 121
Judaism, 98–9, 102
justice, 14, 16, 44, 46, 47, 50–1, 53, 65

Letters of the Living, 115, 118
life after death, 110–14
Local Spiritual Assemblies, 1, 66, 68–70, 71, 72, 77, 131, 132
love, 14–15: of God, 35, 107, 113; physical, 10, 11–12, 14; spiritual, 12, 15, 39, 49, 76, 86, 113

Manifestations (prophet-founders), 93–7, 98–103, 112, 113, 121
marriage, 25–7, 29, 70, 88–9

Mashriqu'l-Adhkár, 74–5, 127, 129
material world: detachment from, 11–12, 78, 84, 88, 97–8, 106, 107, 109–10, 113; enjoyment of, 19; ephemeral nature of, 7; temptations of, 11, 21–2, 105
meditation, 21, 83, 84, 86–7
Mírzá Muhammad 'Alí, 126
moderation, 44, 51
Muhammad, 116, 119

National Spiritual Assemblies, 1, 66, 68–70, 71, 72, 77, 80, 128, 131, 132
Nineteen Day Feast, 67–8
Nine-Year Plan, 128
oneness of religions, 2–3, 57, 75, 96–7, 100, 102, 103

physical health, 23–4, 62, 140: alcohol, 24, 43, 90; drug taking, 24, 43, 63, 90; smoking, 24
prayer, 8, 21, 23, 24, 31, 32, 83, 84, 85, 86, 87, 89, 104
principles and teachings of the Bahá'í Faith: abolitions, 90; administration, 75–82; animals, kindness to, 8, 90; Bahá'í community as a model, 136–40; compassion, 8; Covenant, 77–8; diet, 24; laws, 83–90; minority rights, 81; study of scripture, 84: see also agriculture; chastity; death and burial; divorce; economics; education; environment; equality; family life; fasting; freedom; global perspective; government; happiness and contentment; human rights; humility; Ḥuqúqu'lláh; justice; love; marriage; meditation; moderation; oneness of religions; prayer; purity; science and

technology; service; social teachings; society; spiritual teachings; suffering; truth; unity; women, status of; world peace; worldview

projects for social and economic development, 1, 63–6, 135–6: education projects, 1, 64, 70, 135, 136

publication of Bahá'í literature, 4, 69, 129

purity, 16–17, 78, 85, 105

race issues, 2, 14, 28, 34, 35–7, 62, 63, 70

Regional Spiritual Assemblies, 68

religious persecution and prejudice, 34, 35, 62, 98–9: against Bábís and Bahá'ís, 69, 71, 73, 117–18, 119, 120, 127, 131, 132, 133

science and religion, 40–2, 62, 139

science and technology, 40–2, 65–6

service, 19–20, 29, 39, 51, 58, 79

Seven-Year Plan, 128

Shoghi Effendi, 127–8, 130, 131: and administrative structure of Bahá'í community, 67, 69, 71, 77, 128; appointed leader of Bahá'í Faith, 3, 127; death of, 71, 128; Guardian of the Bahá'í Faith, 3, 127; teachings of, 26, 59, 61–2; writings of, 3, 16, 17, 26, 58, 59, 61, 62, 69, 77, 81, 88, 138–9

Six-Year Plan, 128

social teachings, 2, 14, 15, 25, 27, 32, 34–53, 55, 63–6, 88–9, 102, 129, 135–40

society, 34–53, 63–6

soul, 110, 111, 112, 113–14

spiritual teachings, 2–3, 25, 48, 49, 102: spiritual development, 63, 64, 83–4, 96, 97, 98, 101, 104, 105, 108, 111, 113; spiritual education, 32, 95–6, 108, 112; spiritual health, 23–4, 52–3, 57; spiritual laws, 83,–4 108; spiritual quest, 7–21, 22; spiritual unity, 57, 63

spread of Bahá'í Faith, 4, 68, 71, 124, 127, 128–9, 130–4: see also Five-Year Plan; Four-Year Plan; Nine-Year Plan; Seven-Year Plan; Six-Year Plan; Ten-Year Crusade

suffering, 108–10

Táhirih, 115, 118

Ten-Year Crusade, 128

theological teachings, 91–114: goal of human life, 103–7; intercession for the dead, 114: see also life after death; Manifestations (prophet-founders); God; soul

truth, 8, 15–16, 79

unity, 34, 36, 54–9, 60–2, 63, 64, 65, 75, 76, 78, 79, 81, 83, 85, 88, 102

Universal House of Justice, 3, 40, 70–1, 72, 77–8, 80, 128–9, 130, 131, 137–8, 140

wealth, pursuit of, 5–6, 48, 50–1

women, status of, 2, 28, 35, 37–40, 64, 70, 136, 139, 140: Bahá'í Vocational Institute for Rural Women, 136

world peace, 2, 39, 46, 50, 54, 60, 62, 71, 96, 139

worldview, Bahá'í, 50–1, 54–66: world order, 59–63, 75, 139

Zoroastrianism, 102, 133